JANE ADDAMS
OF HULL HOUSE

Jane Addams

JANE ADDAMS
OF HULL HOUSE
1860-1935

A CENTENARY STUDY

MARGARET TIMS

Ruskin House
GEORGE ALLEN & UNWIN LTD
MUSEUM STREET LONDON

J

Printed in Great Britain
in 11 on 12 pt. Times New Roman type
by East Midland Printing Company Limited
Bury St. Edmunds, Peterborough, Kettering
and elsewhere

CONTENTS

ACKNOWLEDGMENTS

Permission to quote from Jane Addams' published writings is gratefully acknowledged to the following:

Mrs Myra R. Linn—*Democracy and Social Ethics; Newer Ideals of Peace; The Spirit of Youth and the City Streets; The Long Road of Woman's Memory; The Excellent Becomes the Permanent.* The Macmillan Company of New York—*Twenty Years at Hull House; Second Twenty Years at Hull House; A New Conscience and an Ancient Evil; My Friend, Julia Lathrop;* and *Women at The Hague* (Jane Addams, *et al.*).

Women's International League for Peace and Freedom—*Peace and Bread in Time of War.*

Thomas Y. Crowell Company—*Philanthropy and Social Progress* and *Hull House Maps and Papers* (Jane Addams *et al.*).

I am obliged to Appleton-Century-Crofts, Inc., for quotations from *Jane Addams*, by James Weber Linn; Messrs. Allen & Unwin for the extract from *The Transformations of Man*, by Lewis Mumford; Messrs. John Murray for the short excerpt from *Canon Barnett: His Life, Work and Friends*, by Henrietta Barnett; and Messrs. Faber & Faber for the lines quoted from *The Hollow Men*, by T. S. Eliot.

I am immensely indebted to the Women's International League for Peace and Freedom for access to photographs, Congress Reports and many other publications; and to the many members in Britain, the United States of America and Geneva, who have given freely of their information and advice. I should particularly like to thank Mrs Claire Holcomb Walsh of the Jane Addams Centennial Committee in Philadelphia for her helpful co-operation at all stages; and Mrs Florence Pettit for her generous typing assistance.

I am grateful also to the librarian of the Fawcett Society, Westminster, for the provision of books; to the Swarthmore College Peace Collection, Pennsylvania, for material unobtainable in this country; to the Director of Hull House, Chicago, for reports of current activities; and to the Rt. Hon. Lord Pethick-Lawrence of Peaslake for a personal reminiscence of Jane Addams.

The frontispiece photograph was taken at Bar Harbor, Maine, in 1913 by Mr H. J. Koshiba of New York.

September, 1960   M.T.

PART I

THE PATTERN OF LIVING

Chapter 1

1860-1960

THE CENTURY OF PROGRESS

JUST one hundred years ago, on September 6, 1860, a miller's wife in Cedarville, Illinois, gave birth to her eighth child. Two and a half years later Sarah Addams was dead, following the premature birth of a ninth baby precipitated by her over-exertion in helping to deliver a neighbour's wife. Three children of John and Sarah Addams had already died in infancy, and a fourth was to succumb at the age of 16; the ninth baby was born dead.

The eighth child, however, though sickly, survived. She was 'small, frail and pigeon-toed, and carried her head slightly on one side as the result of a slight spinal curvature', her bio-grapher[1] was later to record. She regarded herself as an Ugly Duckling to the point of self-conscious morbidity in early childhood, although a school-friend remembered her as 'a little girl with very pretty, light brown hair'. Chronic ill-health persisted throughout her life and she underwent half a dozen major operations.

In spite of these handicaps Laura Jane Addams, as the child was christened, not only survived but lived to become the most feted, and perhaps most widely-loved, woman of her time. The face of the small, plain child grew to be likened, in maturity, to the 'tragic mask' of Duse: the face of a woman who grew into beauty through her works. The delicate schoolgirl became founder, at the age of twenty-nine, of a pioneer settlement in the Chicago slums that, with Toynbee Hall in London, was to set the pattern for a generation of social work. The diffident young woman, who was never quite sure that she was right, was to oppose a continent at war as leader of the international women's peace movement; to receive fifteen honorary degrees of American universities, the Nobel peace prize and the Greek

medal of military merit; to be reviled as a pacifist and black-
listed as a 'Red'; to have many thousand mourners, both the
humble and the great, file past her coffin in homage.

To what did they pay homage? There were as many choices
as there were human beings. To the internationalist—social
democrat—feminist? The friend of the weak and oppressed?
The lover of youth and beauty?—educator?—administrator?
To the garbage inspector of Ward 19? Or the great 'earth
mother' with a passion for peace and bread? And what, from
this history of both a person and a century, should we remember now?

Lord Pethick-Lawrence has recalled in a letter that Jane
Addams once said to him: 'My grandfather drove his buggy to
the shores of Lake Michigan and looked around him. There
was not a single house then visible where Chicago now stands.'
In 1893 Chicago, already the second city of the United States
although only sixty years old, staged a colossal World's Fair to
commemorate the 400th anniversary of the discovery of
America. The city's own centenary was celebrated in 1933 by a
giant exhibition on the 'Century of Progress'. Both these events,
ironically, took place at a time of financial depression, with
widespread misery and unemployment. The period from 1860,
the year of Jane Addams' birth, to the 'affluent society' of the
present day, may be viewed in many senses as a century of
progress; although progress towards what end, is still uncertain. A century that has encompassed the invention of the
aeroplane and the earth satellite; felt the shattering impact of
Darwin, Marx and Freud; witnessed the phenomena of im-
pressionism, expressionism, surrealism and—realism; this
century does not leave the earth quite as it found it. Never
before in history, we might say, has so much space been com-
pressed into so little time. One world, undoubtedly; but a
world in jeopardy: indissolubly knit together by flash-speed
communications; equally indissolubly tangled by knots of
resistant ideology. How can we undo the knots without cutting
the binding thread?

'The modern world is developing an almost mystic conscious-
ness of the continuity and interdependence of mankind,' wrote
Jane Addams in 1929, in the Introduction to her *Second Twenty
Years at Hull House*, to which she added the corollary:

It lies with us who are here now to make this consciousness—as yet so fleeting and uncertain—the unique contribution of our time to that small handful of incentives which really motivate human conduct.

Thirty years later, as man reaches out to the moon, that consciousness is no less fleeting and uncertain, whilst the need for its development has accelerated a thousandfold. Indeed, the 'mystic' consciousness was characteristic of Jane Addams herself rather than of the modern world to which she then referred. It was one of those subjective necessities about which she wrote so compellingly in her early studies of the social settlement movement in America at the close of the nineteenth century.

She had written also, and with equal conviction, about the objective necessities that determine social change; and there was nothing subjective about her insight into 'that small handful of incentives which really motivate human conduct', or her conclusion that the creation of a world consciousness must be the unique contribution of our time to human evolution. Her insights and conclusions were founded on both experience and observation, upon hard thinking as well as deep emotion, crystallizing in the cold realization, now so clearly evident, that the continuity itself is conditional upon the interdependence of mankind.

In the authoritative *Biography of Jane Addams*, by her nephew James Weber Linn, the author stated his intention to be 'not so much an interpretation of Jane Addams as the story of her life'. She had interpreted herself, he considered, through her own books and particularly in the sentence quoted above. It is the purpose of this present study to carry on where Linn left off, and at least to attempt to bring an interpretation, both of the life and the books, to a new generation of readers. Biographical data are therefore introduced, not necessarily chronologically—except in establishing the pattern of the early years—but as a means of illuminating the historical background and personal character of Jane Addams.

'That small handful of incentives which really motivate human conduct . . .' The more we think about this phrase the more profound it becomes, and, in the complexity and per-

plexity of modern 'civilized' living, the more vital to an understanding of what we are doing on this planet, and why. It would
seem only commonsense to find some satisfactory answer to
these questions before launching on large-scale explorations of
outer space.

In the motivation of human conduct there have been so many
previous explorers, from the first Greek dramatists to the latest
schools of psycho-therapy, that it might seem unnecessary to add
to them. It would be unnecessary, were we living in a properly
integrated society rather than in the fearsome jungle of special-
isms that now threatens to destroy itself. Classical drama is
relegated to the dust-heap of antiquity, psychology to the temple
of the high priests of mammon; neither vehicle of understanding
has its stall in the market-place of daily life. And as the market-
place itself gives way to the super-market, so that 'handful of
incentives' which makes up our human personality is insensibly
manipulated and distorted by the puppet-masters of subliminal
advertising or political propaganda.

Is it not time to call a halt? At least to consider what these
human qualities are and how we can preserve them from
further degradation? To see ourselves whole, in the round, both
as individuals and as members of society, is a vital prerequisite
to the development of the 'world consciousness' on which our
survival depends. There is nothing new in this exercise; it has
been the burden of the poets and philosophers from the dawn
of time. But succeeding epochs must restate, and resolve, their
problems afresh. In any one country or generation only the
very few are ever aware of the real problems; still less of how
to solve them. In an eminent age, Jane Addams joined the
rare company having both awareness and practical application;
the order of Lincoln and Tolstoy, of Gandhi and Albert
Schweitzer.

Her 'intelligence and understanding in social affairs', said
Linn at the time of her death in 1935, rivalled that of Shakes-
peare in his study of the human heart. This was no idle comparison, for besides being her nephew James Linn was Professor
of English at Chicago University. The essay *A Modern Lear*
which Jane Addams wrote out of her experience in the Pullman
strike of 1894 lends some substance to his judgment. It is not
only the depth but the breadth of her understanding that gives

Jane Addams her unique value. In later life, her most passionate concern was for the establishment of lasting peace. She was concerned here not only at the level of political action and international organization, although she never neglected these, but, most characteristically, in a search for the rediscovery of those deeper, more primitive and more potent impulses that motivated human society before the comparatively recent development of large-scale warfare. Not war, but the desire to come to terms with one another, she concluded in *Peace and Bread* shortly after the first World War, is 'the very spring of life which underlies all social organizations and political associations'.

Jane Addams herself never attempted, at any rate in writing, to sum up and draw together in one portmanteau philosophy the broad strands of her thought. Apart from the fact that she continued to work until a few days before her death at the age of seventy-four, and never had the sort of retirement that might have facilitated such an undertaking, it was probably contrary to her nature to lay down for posterity too many hard-and-fast rules or over-riding conclusions. Life was not something to be sorted and packed into a suitcase, or locked away in some mystical casket to which the only key was hidden or lost. Life was rather, for her, a process of unpacking, and the treasures of her wisdom are scattered at random through the close-on fifty years of speech, writing and, not least, action that constituted her public life.

If there is one lesson that Jane Addams reiterated, and exemplified, with unwearying consistency, it is that social progress, education, democracy, ethics, art, religion, peace and, indeed, happiness, must be founded on day-by-day experience. 'Life', she observed in her first and still freshest book, *Democracy and Social Ethics*, 'consists of processes as well as results, and failure may come quite as easily from ignoring the adequacy of one's method as from selfish or ignoble aims'. The sole medium of expression for ethics, she maintained, was *action*. Abstract speculation about morality was no more than observation: 'A situation does not really become moral until we are confronted with the question of what shall be done in a concrete case'. But she was no blundering extrovert; in her youth, indeed, she was given over-much to introspection. She was well aware that action must be preceded by thought, that 'the activities of life can be changed in no other way than by changing the current ideas upon which it is conducted'. [2] And to those who wished to 'change' life for the better, to the do-gooders of whatever persuasion, she had some salutary advice:

A man who takes the betterment of humanity for his aim and end, must also take the daily experiences of humanity for the constant correction of his process. He must not only test and guide his achievement by human experience, but he must succeed or fail in proportion as he has incorporated it with his own. [3]

Jane Addams had the distinction of being, as Walter Lippman expressed it in his obituary notice, 'not only good but great'. The Chicago city council capped this by pronouncing her, after her death (if not always before), 'the greatest woman who ever lived'. Four eminent British gentlemen—Samuel Barnett, John Burns, Sir John Gorst and Sidney Webb—went perhaps one better in giving their united opinion, after meeting her, that Jane Addams 'is the greatest man in America!' Somewhere between these views, no doubt, lies the true measure of her worth as a human being.

There can be no doubt, at any rate, of the greatness of her cause: that of life itself. Here, perhaps, lay her uniqueness: in a wholeness of vision that never mistook the part for the whole; nor forget that the whole is made up of the parts. In this vision, nothing was too great or too small for her attention; nothing was irrelevant or expendable; nothing in life was lost. She had the faculty of transcending the personal without losing sight of the concrete that is the prerogative of the saint and the artist; and Jane Addams was something of both.

She was also something more; or something less, according to the values by which she is judged. In any assessment of Jane Addams it is essential to bear in mind that for her it was not enough to be 'merely' a saint or 'merely' an artist; 'merely' a social reformer, a feminist, or a pacifist. She was all of these things and many others; and each was only an aspect of her overall conception of 'humanity'. First and last, Jane Addams was a human being: one of those vital links in the history of evolution to have added lustre to the name. In her general

aspiration she achieved an almost wholly disinterested manifestation of the human spirit. In the particulars of life that
were so dear to her heart, she inevitably partook of the vision
of a woman—and a most important vision this was to her, but
still no more than a precious contribution to the whole. Her
feminism was never an end in itself, but only a means to enhance
the quality of life all-round. Similarly, her intense sympathy
with the spirit of youth was no sentimental yearning for the
past or vicarious maternal attachment: it sprang from her
clear-sighted knowledge that the future of the race quite
literally belongs to the rising generation.

But who, it may be asked, *was* Jane Addams, and by what
authority does she speak? The self-chosen epitaph on her
tombstone at Cedarville, Illinois, is significant but not in itself
revealing. It reads simply:

JANE ADDAMS of HULL HOUSE and the WOMEN'S
INTERNATIONAL LEAGUE FOR PEACE AND
FREEDOM

What was Hull House? What was the Women's International
League? And what was their connection with Jane Addams
that she should wish to carry it with her to the grave?

Although she confessed herself to be 'very poor' at titles,
there is some illumination in the names of the nine books,
mostly out of print now [4] and little read, that she bequeathed to
a largely unheeding world: *Democracy and Social Ethics* (1902),
Newer Ideals of Peace (1907), *The Spirit of Youth and the City
Streets* (1909), *Twenty Years at Hull House* (1910), *A New
Conscience and an Ancient Evil* (1912), *The Long Road of
Woman's Memory* (1916), *Peace and Bread in time of War*
(1922), *Second Twenty Years at Hull House* (1930), and *The
Excellent Becomes the Permanent* (1932). A tenth book, on
which she was working up to her death, was a biography of a
co-worker, *My Friend: Julia Lathrop* (1935).

These books form the spine of the skeleton, branching out
in innumerable lectures, articles and essays, of which the
Swarthmore College Peace Collection in Pennsylvania has a
complete set. For the flesh and blood we must turn to Linn's
comprehensive biography, already referred to, and to personal
memoirs and correspondence. Taken together, the life and the
records may open a door not only on the past but on the future:

the door by which we came in, and will ultimately go out, leading to 'the continuity and interdependence of mankind'.

In looking more closely at the life of this remarkable woman —from its sober beginnings through perplexity, achievement, recognition and the sufferings of ill-health, opprobrium and isolation, to the final triumphant climax of a national lying-in-state—we can have no better guide for the journey than Jane Addams herself, who in her wisdom has enjoined us to remember:

All the misunderstandings we have in life are due to partial experience, and all life's fretting comes of our limited intelligence. [5]

NOTES

[1] *Jane Addams*, by James Weber Linn (New York, Appleton-Century, 1935), p. 24.
[2] *Peace and Bread in Time of War* (New York, Macmillan, 1922), p. 243.
[3] *Democracy and Social Ethics* (New York, Macmillan, 1902), p. 176.
[4] *Peace and Bread* was re-issued by the Women's International League for Peace and Freedom in 1945 and again in April, 1960.
[5] *Democracy and Social Ethics*, p. 277.

Chapter 2

THE FATHER GOD

JOHN Addams of Cedarville was no ordinary miller, but the town's most respected citizen: a personal friend of Lincoln and a Senator of the Illinois State Assembly for sixteen years. Born at Sinking Springs, Pennsylvania, in 1822, a fourth-generation American of English Quaker ancestry, he became a miller's apprentice and, at the age of twenty-two, married his employer's sister-in-law who was five years his senior. Then began a typical American success story: a ten-days' honeymoon trip to Chicago by way of New York was followed by a further three-months' exploration of the Illinois countryside before John and Sarah Addams settled at the site on the banks of the Cedar River six miles north of Freeport which was to become the family's permanent home.

John Addams' first significant action as a settler in pioneer country was to plant pine trees; his second, to organize the building of a railroad, the Galena & Chicago Union; his third, to rebuild the grist mill he had bought. By the time that the township of Cedarville was laid out in 1849 he was on the way to prosperity. In 1854, at the age of thirty-two, he was elected to the State Senate as a Whig. The following year saw him helping to found the Republican party at Wisconsin, the party for which he was to be returned to office for a further seven terms. Like his daughter after him, higher honours were only denied him by his own lack of political ambition: his refusal to be nominated as Governor of Illinois was to be paralleled half a century later by Jane's refusal to be nominated as candidate for the Presidency of the United States.

The quality, in addition to sheer hard work, that won John Addams the respect of his neighbours was an almost legendary integrity. He was described as the 'king gentleman' of the district. Not only did he never receive a bribe—a rare enough

occurrence at that time and place; he was never offered one.
Years later, Jane could still feel the smart of shame when she
recalled how, in the early days of Hull House, she was offered
50,000 dollars for the Settlement by a manufacturers' association, if she and her colleagues would 'drop this nonsense about
a sweat-shop bill'. Needless to say, the 'nonsense' was not
dropped; but the feeling persisted that somehow she had failed
to measure up to her father's memory.

The probity of John Addams was indeed a formidable
example for an idolatrous small daughter with an exaggerated
moral conscience; particularly so, in the absence of any tem-
pering breeze of maternal sentiment or commonsense. All the
affection and need for identification that in infancy is normally
centred on the mother was in this case, and with a more than
average capacity, transferred to the upright Quaker father:
a kindly, tolerant, but 'not very approachable' man; gentle and
courteous yet always grave and reserved. Jane Addams shared
to a large extent her father's sterner qualities, but her supreme
gift of human sympathy for all sorts and conditions of men,
women and children, appears to have been outside his range.
Was it this fact—the inability to find accord, in this overwhelming 'sympathy', with the one most dear to her—that
caused the later diffusion of her deep affections to embrace the
whole of humanity rather than any other individual being?

In the opening chapter of *Twenty Years at Hull House*, Jane
Addams states clearly the bond that held her to her father: not
only was he the dominant intellectual and moral influence in her
life, which is understandable and not unusual; he was also its
supreme affection. She refers variously to the 'dog-like' and
'adoring' affection she had for him; to her 'great veneration and
pride'; to the desire for identification that caused her to rub
ground wheat between her right forefinger and thumb, in the
hope of flattening it into the semblance of a 'miller's thumb';
and the desire for self-abnegation that led her, ugly duckling as
she supposed herself to be, to attach herself to her uncle's
plainer and less distinguished family rather than 'embarrass'
her imposing father by walking to church beside him. Clearly,
there was no man on earth to touch John Addams; nor ever
would be.

He was a man who put 'mental integrity above everything

else'. And yet, was rectitude for its own sake ever a cardinal virtue? The story of John Addams' response to one mani-festation of his small daughter's conscience is not altogether reassuring. She records how, after telling a lie, she would stay awake for hours torn by a double dread: that she might die herself 'in sin' and go straight to hell; or that her father should die before she told him of her lapse from grace. Finally, she would screw up her courage for the perilous journey down dark stairs, past the street door kept unlocked on principle, and across an empty room to reach the confessional of her father's bedside. His reply was always the same: 'If he had a little girl who told lies, he was very glad that she felt too bad to go to sleep afterwards'. This cold comfort might have been salutary for some children, but to apply it to the over-sensitive Jane betrayed a lack of understanding that she herself was never to repeat in dealing with the hardened young sinners of the Chicago slums. And what unconscious echo was evoked in her adult observation of the 'unlovely result' when 'the entire moral energy of an individual goes into the cultivation of personal integrity'?[1]

This is not to imply that John Addams was not a kind and conscientious father; he was, of course, both. It was scarcely his fault that his 'ugly duckling' should turn out to be a swan of a rather different order than anything yet known in Cedarville, Illinois. He was himself head and shoulders above his neigh-bours in the breadth and depth of his intelligence; a self-styled 'Hicksite Quaker', though never a member of the Society of Friends, who supported with indiscriminate generosity all the churches of the district: a fact that puzzled the youthful Jane and no doubt contributed to her own theological uncertainties. Nor did his Quaker principles prevent him, as a close personal friend of Abraham Lincoln (who used to address him as 'My Dear Double-D'ed Addams'), from actively supporting the Civil War—to the extent of raising and equipping a company which was named the Addams Guard.

The father's hero, *ipso facto*, became the daughter's, and Jane retained a profound admiration for Lincoln, as the emblem of a heroic democracy, all her life. She only came to differ from him, perhaps, in the channels through which she believed that heroism should function; and this digging of new channels was a development of Lincoln's own philosophy rather than a divergence from it. But John Addams' hatred of tyranny and injustice was by no means confined to the American South, and if Jane was to learn on the death of Lincoln that grown-ups too could shed tears, she found her father scarcely less moved at the passing of the Italian patriot Joseph Mazzini. Henceforth, Mazzini too was counted among Jane's heroes.

Already, at the tender age of six, as she tells in her auto-biography, her feeling of responsibility for the 'affairs of the world' was strongly developed:

I dreamed night after night that everyone in the world was dead except myself, and that upon me rested the responsibility of making a wagon-wheel . . . I always stood in the same spot in the deserted blacksmith shop, darkly pondering how to begin, and never once did I know how, although I fully realized that the affairs of the world could not be resumed until at least one wheel should be made and something started . . . The next morning would often find me standing in the doorway of the village blacksmith shop, anxiously watching the blacksmith at work. I would store my mind with such details of the process as I could observe . . . then sigh heavily and walk away, bearing my responsibility as best I could, and of course, confiding it to no one. [2]

This concern with the 'affairs of the world' may be explained, more prosaically, by the proximity of the Addams' home to the working life of the mill which had a great fascination for the child; and the making of bread was to become, both actually and symbolically, one of the twin pillars of Jane Addams' adult philosophy. The other pillar, which does not seem to have stemmed directly from her father, was peace.

At about the same age she caught her first sight of poverty in the back streets of Freeport and felt the rumbling of the social conscience that was to direct her whole future life. Her response to the squalor of these 'horrid little houses' was typical, and showed an almost prophetic insight. When she grew up, she declared, she would live in a big house: but it would be right in the midst of little houses just like these.

It should not be thought, however, that Jane's childhood was all soul-searching and gloomy speculation. Her father's second marriage to Mrs Haldeman—a widow of accomplishment and determination—when she was eight years old does not seem to have diminished her own special relation to him, and it brought her the inestimable gift of a boon companion of her own age. For Mrs Haldeman's two sons were almost of an age with Mr Addams' two younger daughters, a coincidence that was to prove of some significance. Jane seems to have had little in common with her elder sisters Mary and Alice, both of whom went away to Rockford seminary shortly after the advent of the stepmother. But for nine years, until they too were torn apart by boarding school, Jane and her stepbrother George were well nigh inseparable.

Like most women of originality, Jane Addams obtained her larger inspirations from men. George Haldeman was perhaps a little less than inspiring—he committed the unpardonable solecism of scoffing at her social concern (and thereby, who knows, lost a wife?)—but through their expeditions into the countryside she acquired not only a powerful feeling for nature but a scientific interest that led her to consider medicine as a first career. This companionship was important, however, less for the intellectual stimulus of George's lively mind, valuable as this must have been—he was to become a brilliant biological research student—than for the sense it brought for Jane of identification with another human being in an equal relationship; such a sense of equality was impossible with her father, always more God than Man. With her stepbrother she could extend the explorations of one small, solitary soul to an exploration of the outer world, with all the joyous abandon of 'free-ranging country children'. It is this aspect alone of their relationship to which she refers in her autobiographical writings, contrasting it with the 'piteous aspects' of the fragmentary and constantly interrupted recreations of children in the city streets:

We had of course our favorite places and trees and birds and flowers. It is hard to reproduce the companionship which children establish with nature, but certainly it is much too unconscious and intimate to come under the head of aesthetic appreciation or anything of the sort. When we said that the purple wind-flowers—the *anemone patens*—'looked as if the winds had made them', we thought much more of the fact that they were wind-born than that they were beautiful: we clapped our hands in sudden joy over the soft

radiance of the rainbow, but its enchantment lay in our half belief
that a pot of gold was to be found at its farther end; we yielded
to a soft melancholy when we heard the whippoorwill in the early
twilight, but while he aroused in us vague longings of which we
spoke solemnly, we felt no beauty in his call.

We erected an altar beside the stream, to which for several years
we brought all the snakes we killed during our excursions, no
matter how long the toilsome journey which we had to make with
a limp snake dangling between two sticks. I remember rather
vaguely the ceremonial performed upon this altar one autumn day,
when we brought as further tribute one out of every hundred of the
black walnuts which we had gathered, and then poured over the
whole a pitcher full of cider, fresh from the cider mill on the barn
floor. I think we had also burned a favorite book or two upon this
pyre of stones. The entire affair carried on with such solemnity was
probably the result of one of those imperative impulses under
whose compulsion children seek a ceremonial which shall express
their sense of identification with man's primitive life and their
familiar kinship with the remotest past. [3]

Here, as in so many of Jane Addams' reminiscences, are
echoes of something more than childish make-believe: her
feeling, which grew stronger with advancing age, that 'make-
believe' has a much more than childish importance in the
history of the human race. The implication of the passage
quoted is surely that these half-conscious 'intimations of immortality', as Wordsworth had called them, are as natural to
childhood as eating and sleeping; and to deny them their
rightful outlet may be as disastrous in effect as any other kind
of malnutrition.

The claims of formal education were, however, to interrupt
this idyll for Jane and George, and it was never to be renewed.
And with the choice of a school for Jane came the first spark of
rebellion—or at least agnosticism—against the benevolent
despotism of the 'father-god'. Her own ambition was to attend
the famous Smith College on the eastern seaboard, whereas Mr
Addams favoured neighbouring Rockford, which both her
sisters had attended and of which he himself was a Trustee. She
passed for Smith, but the divine will prevailed and she went to
Rockford; at seventeen, she was not yet fledged as a free-
thinker.

Of orthodox religion, though, she had many doubts. She belonged to no church and had never been baptized. This fact strengthened her reluctance for Rockford, which was notorious for its evangelical zeal. Many of the girls became missionaries, or missionaries' wives—there was fruitful co-operation here with the theological students from the nearby Beloit College for boys (where George Haldeman was now a student)—and continual pressure was put on the more able and serious-minded pupils to enter this field of service. Jane recalls that 'the desirability of Turkey as a field for missionary labour was enticingly put before me'. [4] Fortunately for Chicago, if not for Turkey, she resisted this and every other similar appeal, which affected her only with a feeling of acute embarrassment.

She attributed this power of detachment both to the influence of her father, who like herself was not a communicant of any church, and to the rational turn of mind of her own particular group of friends. She was in fact, at this time, relishing the delights of a free-ranging intellect just as she had previously relished a free-ranging exploration of the countryside. The studies at Rockford included Latin, Greek, Natural Science, History and Literature, Mental and Moral Philosophy, and French; the only serious omission, Jane noted, was Economics. She had already received a grounding in history at her father's knee; and if Plutarch's *Lives* and Irving's *Life of Washington* were unusual reading for a juvenile, it is pleasant to be able to report that John Addams rated this labour worthy of a reward of five cents per 'life' and twenty-five cents per volume of Irving! Her school reading included not only Motley and Gibbon but Ruskin, Browning and Carlyle, as well as the Greek and Roman classics, and she retained her interest in Natural Science throughout her school life. But experience gained only from books was chafing to healthy young spirits, and a study of de Quincey's 'dreams' was supplemented by Jane and four other girls with a brief, intensive course of opium; not, however, with any of the hoped-for effects, and the episode ended with an emetic. There was no escape from discipline by that method, and she records the general feeling that 'So much of our time is spent in preparation, so much in routine, and so much in sleep, we find it difficult to have any experience at all'. [5]

Nevertheless, the duckling was flexing its wings, and even a school curriculum could not conceal indefinitely the originality of Jane Addams' unfolding mind. Some of her school essays reveal an astonishing maturity, so that it seemed as if in essentials her philosophy of life was already fixed. Her 'passive resistance' to evangelism was to be the precursor of many similar resistances in later life: resistances to curruption, to war, and to the many forms of 'anarchism' and 'socialism' that threatened the integrity of Hull House with sectarian dogma. And she herself regarded the experience of 'clinging to an individual conviction', against the popular tide of feeling, as the best moral training she received at Rockford. Her conviction even at this stage was not, however, limited to a negative non-co-operation; it was already crystallizing in a positive independence of judgment, as this extract from an oratorical contest clearly shows:

> Those who believe that Justice is but a poetical longing within us, the enthusiast who thinks it will come in the form of a millennium, those who see it established by the strong arm of a hero, are not those who have comprehended the vast truths of life. The actual Justice must come by trained intelligence, by broadened sympathies toward the individual man or woman who crosses our path; one item added to another is the only method by which to build up a conception lofty enough to be of use in the world. [6]

Even as a schoolgirl, her own comprehension of 'the vast truths of life' had outstripped that of the average politician.

Jane's second struggle with the school authorities came over the recognition of her B.A. degree. Although the charter granted to Rockford in 1853 gave its students the right to a college degree, this right had never been exercised; for nearly thirty years Rockford had been content to remain a 'seminary'. Jane was determined that college status should now be achieved, and to this end she and one other student took a course of higher mathematics and she prepared her graduation oration in Greek. There was disapproval of these innovations by the head and some senior staff, but the battle was won in principle—although Jane and her classmate did not actually receive their degrees until the year after their graduation in 1881. And by then, for Jane, the bloom had already faded from the flower of intellectual achievement.

In her graduation oration she had declared, with all the idealism of untested youth:

We stand united today in a belief in beauty, genius and courage, and that these expressed through truest womanhood can yet transform the world. [7]

She never foreswore those ideals; indeed, she largely embodied them. But they were soon to be tempered by the most rigorous tests of practical experience, and she saw in them later a 'sublime self-conceit' and an ignorance of 'the obscure paths of tolerance, just allowance and self-blame wherein, if we held our minds open, we might learn something of the mystery and complexity of life's purposes'. [8]

What happened, to upset so suddenly the confidence in a brilliant future that both her teachers and her classmates must surely have predicted for Jane Addams? In her senior year at Rockford she was riding the crest of the wave: class president, editor of the college magazine (her contributions to which were treated as serious literary criticism by Professor Linn), 'valedictorian' of her year. She had received, and refused, a proposal of marriage from her opposite number at Beloit, the brilliant class president Rollin Salisbury: later to become Professor of Geography at Chicago University, to remain a bachelor—and never to cross the threshold of Hull House.

Long before the end of her schooldays, she records, and in spite of increasing pressure towards a religious vocation, her future life was firmly fixed in her mind: to study medicine and 'live with the poor'. This determination was a mixture of 'veneration for science', then still strong in her, and a Cassandra-like intuition that her fate was 'always to be in the right, and always to be disbelieved and rejected'. Although one part of the prophecy came true, the somewhat inflated philosophy upon which it rested belonged to what she described as the 'rose-coloured mist' of youthful dreams; a mist that was all too quickly to thicken to a very much darker shade.

As Mr T. S. Eliot has expressed it: [9]

Between the idea
And the reality

> Between the motion
> And the act
> Falls the Shadow

What shadow fell, between the graduation ceremony and the attainment of her degree, to throw so promising a life off-course? To what violent trauma, as the psychologists would now call it, was Jane subjected that its effects were to haunt her for the next eight years? She has effectively analysed her own state of mind:

> During most of that time I was absolutely at sea so far as any moral purpose was concerned, clinging only to the desire to live in a really living world and refusing to be content with a shadowy intellectual or aesthetic reflection of it.[10]

The onset of reality, and the consequent shattering of dreams, is a natural part of growth. Its normal course is a gradual unfolding of consciousness, a sloughing-off of the old skin only as the new one is ready to take its place. Jane Addams would in any case have developed beyond the normal span. But only an event of shattering impact could have caused this total rejection of the 'intellectual and aesthetic reflection' in the mirror of life before the image had even been fully envisaged. And in August 1881, just before her twenty-first birthday, the calamity occurred.

Mr and Mrs Addams, accompanied by Jane and George, were then on a trip to the copper-mining region of Lake Superior, where John Addams was surveying certain properties with a view to investment. Here, suddenly, he was seized with a violent internal illness, was rushed back to Green Bay, Wisconsin; and within thirty-six hours was dead. What was, in fact, a burst appendix was diagnosed as 'inflammation of the bowels'; in any case, there was nothing that could be done. He was brought home to Cedarville for burial. Still a comparatively young man, he was fifty-nine years old; his second wife was to survive him until she was over ninety.

Three days later Jane wrote to her school friend Ellen Starr:

The greatest sorrow that can ever come to me has passed, and I hope it is only a question of time until I get my moral purposes straightened.

The letter ended with a warning:

I wish you could come to Cedarville before you return to Chicago, if only for a day or two . . . only prepare yourself so you won't be too disappointed in me when you come.[11]

One wonders how many more people were to be disappointed in Jane Addams at that time, or to understand the circumstances of her apparent deterioration.

This was in fact her second encounter with sudden death that summer. Only a month previously, the district of Freeport had been outraged with the assassination of President Garfield by Julius Guiteau, member of a well-known local family. His father was cashier at John Addams' bank, his half-sister was Jane's chief friend in the town. On the day of his execution, which was carried out in face of his obvious insanity, Jane remained in hiding with her friend to fortify her against both the horror of the hanging and the fury of vengeful neighbours.

The second blow accomplished what the first had only vicariously foreshadowed: the destruction of faith in the benign purposes of life; or indeed, in any purpose whatever. With the death of the father-god—and she had so far known no other— what meaning had life still to offer? It was eight years before an answer came; eight years of seeking, part aimless and part with a half-formed purpose, in which nothing was taken on trust. At twenty-one, Jane Addams became an adult; and started life from scratch. From now on reality must not only, in Keats' phrase, be 'proved on the pulses'; it must be proved on the nerves and sinews, with the acquiescence of brain and muscle as well as of wishful sentiment. Here lay the seeds of that remarkable, slow-flowering wholeness that was to characterize the mature woman, adding depth to the natural breadth of outlook that was to encompass a whole world.

Meanwhile, more as an escape from present sorrows than

from any firm conviction, Jane proceeded with her announced
intention to enter on a course of medical studies.

NOTES

1 *Democracy and Social Ethics*, p. 274.
2 *Twenty Years at Hull House* (New York, Macmillan, 1910), p. 5.
3 *Ibid.*, pp. 17-18.
4 *Ibid.*, p. 50.
5 *Ibid.*, pp. 45-6.
6 *Ibid.*, p. 58.
7 *Jane Addams*, by J. W. Linn., p. 63.
8 *Twenty Years at Hull House*, p. 63.
9 *The Hollow Men*, by T. S. Eliot (London, Faber, 1925).
10 *Twenty Years at Hull House*, p. 64.
11 *Jane Addams*, by J. W. Linn, p. 66.

Chapter 3

SNARES AND DELUSIONS

IN October 1881, accordingly, Jane Addams registered as a
student at the Women's Medical College of Philadelphia. She
remained there seven months. Study as she may, and she passed
all her first year subjects with credit, her heart was no longer,
if it had ever been, in the profession of medicine. This forcing
of herself against the grain, coupled with the nervous shock of
her father's death, brought on a recurrence of spinal trouble,
and she was obliged to enter hospital in Philadelphia the
following spring. As soon as she was well enough to travel, she
returned to Cedarville.

Bereaved of its miller, the beloved mill-house was no cure. Her
condition became worse and the following winter she was bed-
bound at the home of her sister Alice in Iowa, where she remained almost a complete invalid, for six months. Why, one
wonders, in Iowa and not in Cedarville? The suspicion is
inescapable that this further retreat from 'reality' was largely a
retreat from the importunities of a strong-willed stepmother.
Looking back on life at the age of seventy in the *Second Twenty
Years at Hull House*, Jane Addams was to describe the influence
of old women, in a moment of rare bitterness, as a 'social
menace'. The relation between Jane and her stepmother hardly
gave scope for 'menace', but there was a temperamental barrier
between them that must have been as tedious to the young
woman as it was vexatious to the elder. One aspect of this block
to understanding was Mrs Addams' tirelessness in match-
making between Jane and George, although ironically, the
marriage between Alice Addams and her elder son Harry, which
had taken place five years previously, was violently opposed
by both parents.

Harry Haldeman seems to have been a somewhat erratic
character, of brilliant accomplishment but little scruple. Never-

theless, in his younger days, he was a noted surgeon, and during Jane's stay he performed an operation to correct her spinal curvature. She convalesced, encased in a metal straight-jacket that she was to wear for more than a year, with Carlyle's *Frederick the Great*, and records her gratitude that it was not Gray's *Anatomy*. But there were less grateful thoughts to dwell on in that long, inactive winter with the knowledge, revealed to her at this time by Dr Haldeman, that it would never be possible for her to bear a child. The fact is recorded briefly in Linn's biography and nowhere referred to in her own published writings. She was twenty-two, still largely unformed; it is impossible to know how decisive a factor this knowledge was to be in her consistent disregard of marriage. But it is reasonable to assume that to the woman who, more than any other, was to become the symbol of universal motherhood, a marriage without children would be little more than a travesty.

Meanwhile, as an antidote to depression, a trip to Europe was prescribed. In August 1883, just two years after her father's death, Jane embarked, with her stepmother and a party of friends, on what was to be a momentous tour. Their first stop was Ireland, and Jane records, in the inevitable young lady's 'journal', a typical comment; 'Could not kiss the Blarney stone, though the Castle is very beautiful'. It was an accomplishment she never learned, but this particular abstention was linked to her observation that the owner of Blarney Castle had an income of £13,000 a year, whereas the 'ordinary man' had six shillings a week. Again, driving through the beautiful Irish countryside, she noted the poverty of the land and the mean houses, many without windows; but noted too, that the people were healthy and long-lived. There is always a mitigating picturesqueness to take the edge off Irish squalor.

Not so in London, which the party reached after two months tourism extend from Scotland to Stratford-on-Avon. In the Mile End Road, Jane received her first real taste of the horrors of city poverty, with all its attendant miseries, when she was taken by a missionary to one of the regular Saturday night auctions held there to dispose of the rotting fruit and vege-tables that could not be trusted to 'keep' over the weekend.

On Mile End Road, from the top of an omnibus which paused at the end of a dingy street lighted by only occasional flares of gas, we saw two huge masses of ill-clad people clamoring around two hucksters' carts. They were bidding their farthings and ha'pennies for a vegetable held up by the auctioneer, which he at last scornfully flung, with a gibe for its cheapness, to the successful bidder. In the momentary pause, only one man detached himself from the groups. He had bidden in a cabbage, and when it struck his hand, he instantly sat down on the curb, tore it with his teeth, and hastily devoured it, unwashed and uncooked as it was. [1]

Her final impression, of 'myriads of hands, empty, pathetic, nerveless and workworn, showing white in the uncertain light of the street, and clutching forward for food which was already unfit to eat', was to haunt her for years.

I have never since been able to see a number of hands held upward, even when they are moving rhythmically in a calisthenic exercise, or when they belong to a class of chubby children who wave them in eager response to a teacher's query, without a certain revival of this memory, a clutching at the heart reminiscent of the despair and resentment which seized me then. [2]

Jane Addams' immediate reaction is also interesting. Why should the sight of poverty fill her with 'resentment and despair'? Why should she thereafter walk through London afraid to look down narrow streets 'lest they disclose again this hideous human need and suffering'? Why should she suddenly feel that 'all huge London' is unreal, except the poverty of the East End (the like of which she was to find in no other country of Europe)? The despair is readily explained by her knowledge that she could do nothing to alleviate the misery (she was not then aware, as she later records, of the many schemes of municipal reform already being prepared); and what she resented was the knowledge that she was not *expected* to do anything—had she tried, her state of health would certainly have given serious cause for alarm!

As a young woman of culture with pretensions to learning, the conventional purpose of her European tour was the acquisition of more culture and greater learning. For young Americans, this was a regular thing to do, and amongst girls at any rate, it is doubtful if its value had been seriously questioned before.

To Jane Addams, however, the prospect laid more and more heavily on her spirit, burdened as it was beginning to be by the *Weltschmertz* of poverty. As the tour proceeded, the feeling of futility—or worse, of *mis-directed* energy—grew wellnigh intolerable, and she reached the conclusion that 'the pursuit of culture would not, in the end, bring either solace or relief'. Her blackest gall sprang from the general assumption that 'the sheltered, educated girl has nothing to do with the bitter poverty and social maladjustment which is all about her'; that same girl who was destined to become as a woman—in Jane Addams' almost religious conviction—the guardian and 'chief nourisher' of the human race! How much more testing could her preparation be?

In Saxe-Coburg she was to watch, with mounting indignation, the female brewery workers carrying wooden tanks of scalding liquid fastened to their backs:

The women were bent forward, not only under the weight which they were bearing, but because the tanks were so high that it would have been impossible for them to have lifted their heads. Their faces and hands, reddened in the cold morning air, showed clearly the white scars where they had previously been scalded by the hot stuff which splashed if they stumbled ever so little on their way. [3]

On this occasion, indignation was translated into action, and she hurried over to interview the owner of the brewery, who received her with 'exasperating indifference'. She returned to her hotel with little appetite either for breakfast or for her current reading of Gray's *Life of Prince Albert*.

In Dresden she went the rounds of the art galleries and opera, always with the same after-effect of 'moral revulsion'. This revulsion was not caused by any lack of aesthetic appreciation in Jane Addams. Rather, she had to steel herself against the drug of beauty, constantly, to remind herself of the conditions of 'real life' that were, so often, in hideous contrast to the classical works of art. She had a particularly keen responsiveness to architecture which found an affinity in the structure of the 'cathedral', a concept that was to recur in differing forms throughout her life. She was deeply moved too, by the drawings of Dürer; though less as works of art, she admits, than as 'human documents':

I was chiefly appealed to by his unwillingness to lend himself to a smooth and cultivated view of life, by his determination to record its frustrations and even the hideous forms which darken the day for our human imagination and to ignore no human complications. [4]

This first European tour lasted twenty-one months and included the British Isles, Holland, Germany, Austria, Italy, Greece and Switzerland, culminating in a two-months stay in Berlin and a final visit to Paris. How many young women of twenty-three had such an opportunity? But exclusiveness only added to the guilt of privilege. The experience, for all its moments of inspiration, brought no lasting satisfaction. The most she could say was that 'the wonder and beauty of Italy later brought healing and some relief to the paralysing sense of the futility of all artistic and intellectual effort when disconnected from the ultimate test of the conduct it inspired'. [5] Nevertheless, the tour was by no means a dead loss. Almost in spite of herself, she absorbed the best of European culture through its languages, history and philosophy. Nor did she fail in relating her knowledge to the 'ultimate test' of conduct, as she struggled to express her still unrealized convictions in the continuous outpouring of her private notebooks. But she returned to Cedarville, her biographer records, 'spiritually more confused than when she left it'.

The next two years registered the low-water mark both of aspiration and achievement. What had happened to the budding talent? It stubbornly refused to flower, inhibited as any work of nature is by an uncongenial habitat. Having the properties of the oak rather than the orchid, the genius of Jane Addams wilted and grew pale in the mildly hot-house climate of American provincial society. The winters were spent in Baltimore where George Haldeman was now studying for his doctorate at the Johns Hopkins University; and where George went, there went Jane and the indomitable Mrs Addams, still obtusely intent on a 'match'. She can have had little inkling of her step-daughter's qualities. In the summer, the family returned to their old home at Cedarville.

C

It was in Baltimore, Jane records, that she reached 'the nadir of my nervous depression and sense of maladjustment'. The company of George seems to have lost its savour, at any rate on her side; although he himself was a not unwilling accomplice of Mrs Addams, and as the suit refused to prosper he took refuge finally in a nervous breakdown, from which he never fully recovered. What Jane's true feelings were remains undisclosed; but she was by then as out of sympathy with pure science as he, on his side, was out of sympathy with her social concern. The halcyon days of childhood confidence between them were gone for ever, and no new basis developed for a continuing relationship. This must have been a bleak period for both of them, but George had at least the solace of his work. For Jane, the brash young scientists of the university offered no compensation, and she was frankly bored by the social round of small talk and soirees that bounded her stepmother's horizon. Her only comfort at this time seems to have been derived from a course of lectures on archaeology and a study of the United Italy movement—both being subjects which she could, and did, relate to the living social condition. But their net result was only to add to the dissatisfaction of her own vicarious experience and her disillusionment with 'the effect of intellectual pursuits upon moral development'.

In Illinois, things were slightly better. At least there was more real activity here, and more to be learned from the life of the local people. She was even able to do a little social investigation, and was horrified to discover the wretched condition of the farmers in an area of Kansas where, on the advice of Harry Haldeman, now turned banker, she had invested some money in 'chattel mortgages':

A number of starved hogs—collateral for a promissory note—were huddled into an open pen. Their backs were humped in a curious, camel-like fashion, and they were devouring one of their own number, the latest victim of absolute starvation or possibly merely the one least able to defend himself against their voracious hunger. The farmer's wife looked on indifferently, a picture of despair as she stood in the door of the bare, crude house, and the two children behind her, whom she vainly tried to keep out of sight, continually thrust forward their faces almost covered by masses of coarse, sun-burned hair, and their little bare feet so black, so hard, the great cracks so filled with dust that they looked like flattened hoofs. The children could not be compared to anything so joyous as satyrs, although they appeared but half-human. [6]

She promptly withdrew her investment, with more impetuosity than logic, since she remarks that the farmers doubtless suffered hardship. But characteristically, her action did not stop at this negative gesture. With the money refunded she bought a farm near her own village. Her partner in this venture was an unnamed young college student, and she records the result of their joint enterprise with admirable detachment:

This pastoral enterprise still seems to me to have been essentially sound, both economically and morally, but perhaps one partner depended too much upon the impeccability of her motives and the other found himself too preoccupied with study to know that it is not a real kindness to bed a sheepfold with straw, for certainly the venture ended in a spectacle scarcely less harrowing than the memory it was designed to obliterate. At least the sight of two hundred sheep with four rotting hoofs each, was not reassuring to one whose conscience craved economic peace. [7]

The farm was sold as speedily as it had been acquired and the partners went their separate ways, one back to college—the other back to Europe.

One other event of significance occurred before this second trip. In the summer of 1885, when she was twenty-five years old, Jane Addams was baptized as a member of the Presbyterian Church. This step was the result neither of outside pressure nor inner compulsion, beyond a rather vague feeling of the need for 'an outward symbol of fellowship'. Indeed, it signalled a defeat rather than a victory of the spirit, based on the admission that 'various cherished safeguards and claims to self-dependence had been broken into by many piteous failures'. [8] Perhaps she was still remembering that her father had never submitted to any creed. There was, however, a positive aspect of her admission to the church, in her increasing identification of the faith of the early Christians with the ideals of democracy: ideals for which she was beginning to feel 'an almost passionate devotion'. Her motives were certainly more social than religious, and their implementation was made easier by the tolerance of the local young clergyman who did not force her assent to unpalatable dogmas.

At the time of her second sailing for Europe, Jane Addams was twenty-seven, with a private income of 3,000 dollars a year —and still undecided what to do with her life. Sick as she was with intellectual pursuits, she had retained her general interest in education to the extent of presenting Rockford College with a thousand dollars for science books as her first gift from the estate inherited from her father, and she consented to become a trustee of the college as he had been. She helped two young men with their college fees, and indulged in innumerable other generosities. She also assisted, both financially and with personal service, the growing family of her eldest sister Mary, who had married a Presbyterian Minister; and on Mary's early death, in 1894, she was to assume guardianship of the youngest child, then a boy of ten. But all this estimable work for others hardly constituted a career, as she herself was only too pain-fully aware. She was free, independent, and physically as strong as she would ever be: why then this intolerable feeling of frustration, isolation and uselessness? No doubt the knowledge that she could never have a family of her own fortified her natural sympathies in directing her thoughts more than a young woman commonly would towards the wider community of human society. She could not forget that beyond Baltimore lay not only Greece and Rome, but the Mile End Road. Her school-friend Ellen Starr was already in Europe and in Decem-ber, 1887, Jane packed her bags and followed, accompanied this time not by her stepmother, but by another friend, Sarah Anderson.

This second European tour was to prove very different from the first, in both its immediate experiences and its far-reaching effects. For one thing, there was the difference in her own status. She travelled on alone from Paris to Munich, and notes with satisfaction that she is now addressed as 'Madame', and that 'I felt perfectly at my ease all the time'. On the way she stopped to visit the cathedral at Ulm, and here she caught the first glimpse of her future vision of 'a cathedral of humanity . . . capacious enough to house a fellowship of common purposes and . . . beautiful enough to persuade men to hold fast to the vision of human solidarity'. [9] She sat up half the night recording this waking dream in her notebook: the first fragment of solid masonry on which the whole edifice of her future life was to be built.

But the pattern was still not fully traced out, and the following spring found the three friends established in Rome and 'settled into a certain student's routine'. For Jane, this meant a study of the Catacombs and the history of the early Christians. Then, as was so often to happen, her programme was abruptly terminated at the end of a fortnight by the onset of illness: a severe attack of sciatic rheumatism reduced her to a state of invalidism for several weeks. As soon as she could travel she left for the Riviera, her friends having preceded her to southern Italy at her own insistence. She was paying half the expenses for all of them. From there, in April 1888, they arrived in Spain. And it was in Madrid, on Easter Day, that the long dormant seed was suddenly to fructify and the building of the 'cathedral of humanity' to begin.

The occasion was, of all things, a bull-fight—to which a party of five friends had gone, no doubt in ignorance of the real nature of the spectacle. The other four left early but Jane remained, entranced by the 'glories of the amphitheatre', while five bulls were killed. She confessed afterwards that she had not thought much about the bloodshed. She had seen the slaughter through the romantic haze of a knightly tournament. Conventional morality never sat easily on Jane Addams' conscience, and her instinctive response was always to the poetic rather than the outward truth. Nevertheless, her imaginative transformation of the bull-fight was a distortion by any standards and once outside the arena—where her friends waited 'stern and pale with disapproval'—she was soon overcome with disgust. As usual, the revulsion rebounded on herself. Her failure to perceive the reality of the bull-fight she saw as the inevitable corollary of her whole way of life:

It was suddenly made quite clear to me that I was lulling my conscience by a dreamer's scheme, that a mere paper reform had become a defence for continued idleness, and that I was making it a *raison d'etre* for going on indefinitely with study and travel . . . I had fallen into the meanest type of self-deception in making myself believe that all this was in preparation for great things to come.[10]

From now on, she resolved, 'the plan' would be translated
into action. For indeed a plan did exist, and a far more explicit
one than she had so far dared to admit to another human being.
She had already been thinking about it, even before this second
trip to Europe, and in essentials it was to be carried out almost
exactly as laid down in her own still groping mind:

I gradually became convinced that it would be a good thing to rent
a house in a part of the city where many primitive and actual needs
are found, in which young women who had been given over too
exclusively to study, might restore a balance of activity along
traditional lines and learn of life from life itself; where they might
try out some of the things they had been taught and put truth to
'the ultimate test of the conduct it dictates or inspires'. [11]

In the execution of this plan she was inhibited, not by any
lack of precision in her own ideas, but by lack of confidence
that they would receive sympathetic hearing: she had had
little encouragement to think so in her own family. But now
she could hold back no longer, and the day following the
bull-fight she broached the subject to Ellen Starr:

I told it in the fear of that disheartening experience which is so apt
to afflict our most cherished plans when they are at last divulged,
when we suddenly feel that there is nothing there to talk about, and
as the golden dream slips through our fingers, we are left to wonder
at our own fatuous belief. [12]

She scarcely dared to hope that Miss Starr, herself an artist,
might join her in carrying out the scheme. To her delighted
astonishment, her friend was not only willing to participate,
but enthusiastic. With this encouragement, the worst hurdle
was over. It only remained to find the ways and means; and
from now on, everything conspired for success.

The following month found Jane Addams in London, and in
a very different mood from that despair and resentment of five
years previously. Released into activity, she was now less
conscious of the overwhelming misery than of the many efforts
being made for alleviation and reform. She attended a strike
meeting of the London match girls in protest against low wages,
and the dangerous use of phosphorus in the industry which

gave rise to the disease of 'phossy jaw', although she admits that she did not at that time have any real understanding of trade unionism or the labour movement. She studied the socialism of William Morris, the Webbs and the young Bernard Shaw, then launching his first deadly missiles against complacency in the tracts of the newly-formed Fabian Society. She attended lectures on Positivism, to which she was greatly attracted as prefiguring the kind of universalism she was later to find in the World Fellowship of Faiths.

Above all, she was impressed by the work of the East End Settlement, Toynbee Hall, which had been founded in Whitechapel by a group of Oxford men four years earlier. It was this link with the university that gave her a vital clue for the working of her own scheme to bring American college women into a more useful and mutually beneficial relation with the harsher realities of life. In June 1888, she presented herself to its warden, Rev Samuel (later Canon) Barnett, in what was to be the first of several interchanges on both sides of the Atlantic.

On this occasion, the visit was a brief one. She was 'raring' to be off, eager now to get back to her own people and begin her rightful work. The old reasons for delay had miraculously vanished: she was no longer alone and unrecognized, confiding only to the secrecy of her notebook: she was not after all a 'crank' or an oddity, making fantasy the excuse for inaction. She had been right to wait until the dream could be seen as a practical, living reality that was taken seriously by practical, living human beings. Without the example of Toynbee Hall, it is doubtful if Hull House would ever have been founded: its coming would certainly have been delayed, and further delay at that climatic moment might well have dealt a death-blow to Jane Addams' larger hopes.

She was to call this period of her life, in Tolstoy's phrase, 'the snare of preparation', and she deplored the adult attitude towards young people of 'hopelessly entangling' them in inactivity at the time when they were most anxious to 'construct the world anew'. In fact the entanglement was, and usually is, an inner one that could be unravelled only by the growth of self-understanding. It is doubtful if the particular snares encountered by Jane Addams could have been avoided, or the period of preparation shortened, in any circumstances: nor would her achievement have been greater if they had. Youthful attempts to 'construct the world anew', if carried out at all, are usually as abortive as they are ill-conceived. To a character of Jane Addams' calibre, nothing was lost by waiting except a few years of unhappiness that were more than counterbalanced by the compensating access of wisdom. In the years between twenty-one and twenty-eight, she journeyed further towards understanding than most people in a lifetime.

NOTES

[1] *Twenty Years at Hull House*, p. 67.
[2] *Ibid.*, p. 68.
[3] *Ibid.*, p. 74.
[4] *Ibid.*, p. 75.
[5] *Ibid.*, p. 76.
[6] *Ibid.*, pp. 79-80.
[7] *Ibid.*, pp. 80-81.
[8] *Ibid.*, p. 78.
[9] *Ibid.*, p. 83.
[10] *Ibid.*, p. 86.
[11] *Ibid.*, p. 85.
[12] *Ibid.*, p. 87.

PART II

ETHICS AND INSTITUTIONS

Chapter 4

THE BIG HOUSE

JANE Addams had not forgotten her childish vision of a big house set among a lot of little ones, and the new year found her scouring the slums of Chicago in search of such a property. One day she noticed 'a fine old house, standing well back from the street, surrounded on three sides by a broad piazza which was supported by wooden pillars of exceptionally pure Corinthian design and proportion'[1]; but, failing to take note of its exact situation, she could not find the place again.

Three weeks later, on the advice of the Mayor of Chicago who had been sympathetic to the scheme from the start, a location was recommended near the junction of Blue Island Avenue, Halsted Street and Harrison Street. And in this triangle, it turned out, was the house with the wooden pillars: No 335 (now 800) South Halsted Street, at the junction of Polk Street, known as Hull House in memory of the pioneer citizen Charles J. Hull who built it for his home thirty years earlier. It had since been used at various times as a factory, a furniture warehouse, and a home for the aged; and it was still partly occupied by the offices and storeroom of an adjoining factory. It stood, quite literally, between drink and death: at one side of the house was an undertaker's; and at the other, a saloon.

In September, 1889, Jane Addams and Ellen Starr, together with a housekeeper, took over quarters on the first and second floors; and the following spring the owner of the house, Miss Helen Culver, generously offered a free leasehold of the whole premises until 1920.

The setting of Hull House at the time of their occupation is best described in Jane Addams' own words:

Halsted Street is thirty-two miles long, and one of the great thoroughfares of Chicago; Polk Street crosses it midway between the stockyards to the south and the ship-building yards on the north branch of the Chicago River. For the six miles between these two industries the street is lined with shops of butchers and grocers, with dingy and gorgeous saloons, and pretentious establishments for the sale of ready-made clothing. Polk Street, running west from Halsted Street, grows rapidly more prosperous; running a mile east to State Street, it grows steadily worse, and crosses a network of vice on the corners of Clark Street and Fifth Avenue. Hull House once stood in the suburbs, but the city has steadily grown up around it and its site now has corners on three or four foreign colonies. Between Halsted Street and the river live about ten thousand Italians —Neapolitans, Sicilians and Calabrians, with an occasional Lombard or Venetian. To the south on Twelfth Street are many Germans, and side streets are given over almost entirely to Polish and Russian Jews. Still farther south, these Jewish colonies merge into a huge Bohemian colony, so vast that Chicago ranks as the third Bohemian city in the world. To the northwest are many Canadian-French, clannish in spite of their long residence in America, and to the north are Irish and first-generation Americans. On the streets directly west and farther north are well-to-do English-speaking families, many of whom own their houses and have lived in the neighbourhood for years; one man is still living in his old farmhouse. [2]

For the rendering of Jane Addams' experimental philosophy, could there have been a better crucible? From the start, Hull House was a microcosm of the larger world. Of the total population of Chicago, already approaching one million, nearly three-quarters at that time were foreign-born. In the immediate district of Hull House—the fourteenth precinct of Ward nineteen of the city, with its 50,000 inhabitants—the human spectrum presented some of its darkest shades. The thousands of newly-arrived immigrants were mostly as ignorant of civic duties as they were of their rights as American citizens, while the older residents were only intent on getting out of the district altogether. In such a ward, Jane Addams commented, the whole idea of self-government was liable to break down:

The streets are inexpressibly dirty, the number of schools inadequate, sanitary legislation unenforced, the street lighting bad, the paving miserable and altogether lacking in the alleys and smaller streets, and the stables foul beyond description . . . Rear tenements flourish; many houses have no water-supply save the faucet in the back yard, there are no fire-escapes, the garbage and ashes are placed in wooden boxes which are fastened to the street pavement. [3]

Most of the houses were small, wooden erections, grossly over-crowded, with a few larger tenements and an abundance of the home 'sweat shops' of the clothing industry. In Ward nineteen there were seven churches, two missions and 255 drinking saloons: one saloon to every twenty-eight voters.

Into this great seething, savoury stewpot of humanity stepped Miss Addams and Miss Starr, armed only with their college degrees, their courage and enthusiasm, and the sympathetic support of a handful of well-wishers. The enterprise was started out of their own personal resources and they issued no financial appeals. The 'idea' of the settlement had grown from the example of Toynbee Hall. Its 'objective value', in the con-ditions of the neighbourhood, scarcely needed underlining, although Jane Addams gave chapter and verse in a paper on that theme delivered at the summer school of the Ethical Culture Societies in 1892; and at the same time, perhaps, removed a misconception. For she made it quite clear why the site of Hull House was chosen: it was because of 'its diversity and the variety of activity for which it presented an opportunity'. There were no trained social workers in 1889, and the first Hull House residents did not come as reformers; they came simply as human beings, as eager to learn from their neighbours as they were to teach, and thereby create a fuller life for all. The reasons quoted are a literal statement of fact, with no moral overtones.

But facts arising from conscious choice are not mere accidents of circumstance; they are the result of an act of will. And why, 'in fact', it may be wondered, should these two cultured young women, well-endowed both in status and in natural gifts, choose out of all the world to live on Halsted Street? It was strange indeed—the 'strangest thing he had met', in the ex-perience of one old Irish neighbour—but to Jane Addams and her co-workers it was no more than natural: they came to Hull House because that was where they wanted to be. And those who did not want to be there, she considered, had better stay away: the first essential for successfully living amongst the poor was a 'genuine preference for residence in an industrial quarter to any other part of the city, because it is interesting and makes the human appeal'.[4]

To understand the insistence of this want, and the level at which it operated at any rate for Jane Addams herself, it is necessary to explore her philosophy a little further. She went a good way towards explaining it, with the wealth of imaginative detail that she brought to all her findings, in another paper at that same ethical summer school, entitled 'The Subjective Necessity for Social Settlements'. In this, she traced the three main trends of the settlement movement: firstly, the desire to add 'the social function' to political democracy; secondly, to assist in the general progress of the race; and thirdly, as an expression of Christianity through humanitarian activity.

Both in America and in England, where the movement had started—out of a greater need, suggested Jane Addams, due to the more rigid British educational and class system—the whole concept of the social settlement came from the top. It was in no sense due to popular pressure against intolerable con-ditions—an impossibility at the level of destitution—but was rather a voluntary renunciation by a privileged minority of its favoured position in society: a small revolution by consent rather than by coercion. But the interesting thing is that there was an element of coercion too: though voluntary workers were not 'conscripted' into settlements, they were most defin-itely impelled there. The 'subjective necessity' pertained to the leaders of the movement, not to the people they served; al-though the benefits were, of course, mutual. It was because she had found her own position intolerable that Jane Addams opened Hull House; and that hundreds flocked to join her. She was the standard-bearer for a generation that had lost its moral worthiness; and thereby lost its own sense of worthiness to live: a lesson of history, as will be seen later, that we still have not learned. She was speaking not only for herself when she said on this occasion:

We have in America a fast-growing number of cultivated young people who have no recognized outlet for their active faculties. They hear constantly about the great social maladjustment, but no

way is provided for them to change it, and their uselessness hangs
about them heavily . . . These young people have had advantages
of college, of European travel, and of economic study, but they are
sustaining this shock of inaction . . . Many of them dissipate
their energies in so-called enjoyment. Others not content with that,
go on studying and go back to college for their second degree; not
that they are especially fond of study, but because they want something definite to do, and their powers have been trained in the
direction of mental accumulation. Many are buried beneath this
mental accumulation with lowered vitality and discontent . . . This
young life, so sincere in its emotion and good phrases and yet so
undirected, seems to me as pitiful as the other great mass of destitute
lives. One is supplementary to the other, and some method of communication can surely be devised. [5]

This yearning to give some social reality to the theories of
democracy was a general, and often a fairly superficial, one; for
the majority, perhaps, it was satisfied by a little *bonhomie* around
the camp fire or the Christmas tree. But Jane Addams traced
back its source to the very roots of humanity; and without
sustenance from the roots, she perceived, the most exquisite
flowers of the intellect would wither and perish:

There is something primordial about these motives, but I am perhaps
overbold in designating them as a great desire to share the race
life. [6]

Nevertheless, share it she must, and we must, if we are to
survive:

You may remember the forlorn feeling which occasionally seizes
you when you arrive early in the morning a stranger in a great city:
the stream of laboring people goes past you as you gaze through the
plate-glass window of your hotel; you see hard working men lifting
great burdens; you hear the driving and jostling of huge carts and
your heart sinks with a sudden sense of futility. The door opens
behind you and you turn to the man who brings you in your breakfast with a quick sense of human fellowship. You find yourself
praying that you may never lose your hold on it all. A more poetic
prayer would be that the great mother breasts of our common
humanity, with its labor and suffering and its homely comforts, may
never be withheld from you. [7]

There was, however, nothing sentimental about Jane Addams'
vision of the common man, as she was to prove later in her
handling of the labour unions; any more than the Christian
humanitarianism was sentimental which prompted men to
express their faith in action by means of social service. For Jane,
Christianity was one of a number of ethical impulses which
could be confined neither to a particular creed nor to a set form
of activity:

The Settlement movement is only one manifestation of that wider
humanitarian movement which throughout Christendom, but pre-
eminently in England, is endeavouring to embody itself, not in a
sect, but in society itself. [8]

Above all, she concluded, the settlement must maintain its
flexibility and tolerance; a tolerance based not on sloppiness
or indifference but on the patient accumulation of facts and the
steady holding of sympathies:

It must be grounded in a philosophy whose foundation is on the
solidarity of the human race, a philosophy which will not waver
when the race happens to be represented by a drunken woman or an
idiot boy . . . the highest moralists have taught that without the
advance and improvement of the whole, no man can hope for any
lasting improvement in his own moral or material individual condition; and that the subjective necessity for Social Settlements is
therefore identical with that necessity, which urges us on toward
social and individual salvation. [9]

Here was the clarion call that within a few years was to
resound, with astonishing repercussions, throughout America.
The first American settlement had actually preceded Hull House
by three years: that founded in New York in 1886 by Dr Stanton
Coit of the Ethical Society. By 1900 the number has risen above
a hundred; and by 1911, no less than four hundred settlements
flourished in the United States. All this activity could be traced
back to the influence of Toynbee Hall, for Dr Coit, like Jane
Addams, had been impressed by the work of the Whitechapel
settlement and had spent three months in residence there before
starting his East Side Neighborhood Guild.

It is perhaps of interest to compare the stated objects of the early British and American settlements. The Universities Settlement Association (of Oxford and Cambridge), established in 1884, laid down as its first aim:

To provide education and the means of recreation and enjoyment for the people in the poorer districts of London and other great cities; to enquire into the condition of the poor and to consider and advance plans calculated to promote their welfare.

Other clauses of the memorandum dealt with the provision of premises and staff; and of funds for salaries and maintenance. The Hull House Charter, incorporated in 1895, gave its objects as being:

To provide a center for a higher civic and social life; to institute and maintain educational and philanthropic enterprises; and to investigate and improve the conditions in the industrial districts of Chicago.

From the start, these aims developed chronologically one out of another, as the awareness of need extended from the stark, human evidence of poverty to a consideration of its causes and cure. If the emphasis at Hull House, as distinct from Toynbee Hall, was firstly on the provision of a centre and only secondly on an educational programme, this reflected less a difference of intention than the differing approach of, on the one hand, a group of university clerics and on the other, a woman of devouring human sympathies. To Jane Addams herself, to her fellow workers, and to the thousands who came and went through its hospitable doors, Hull House was always a home for people to be in, rather an institution for the achievement of a particular kind of work.

In practice, of course, because the women who founded it were equipped with heads as well as hearts, it was both. And the first organized activity, a weekly reading group on George Eliot's *Romola* conducted by Ellen Starr, set the tone for what proved to be the most popular type of 'class': that combining an effort of serious study with a background of social relaxation. The reading party led naturally to the formation of a variety of social clubs catering for the differing needs of young

D

people and old, of men and women, and for the many nationalities to whom Hull House was their first real contact with
American democracy in action.

Sir Walter Besant had warned Jane Addams at the start
not to make Hull House too educational; although it might be
easier to develop a 'polytechnic institute' than a recreational
centre, he doubted whether the former was as useful. Since she
believed passionately in recreation as a means of 're-creation',
Jane was unlikely to fall into that error. Had she not started
her venture in partnership with a practising artist? And was
not the first public building to be added to Hull House an art
gallery? To be followed within a few years by a music school
and little theatre? Classes in arts and crafts conducted by
professionals, exhibitions and performances, Sunday concerts,
choirs and orchestras were soon to be a regular feature of life
on Halsted Street with all the rich heritage of imported European
culture to draw upon at its own doorstep. Here, if in no other
way, was Jane Addams' claim justified that life in a settlement
had more to offer, to all manner of men and women, at that
particular intersection of time and place, than could easily
be found in any other industrial city of the world.

The art gallery was opened in 1891 by Samuel Barnett and his
wife, then travelling through America on a world tour; a similar
gallery was to be established in Whitechapel ten years later.
That same year, 1891, saw the opening also of a public kitchen
at Hull House, with the object of providing cheap and nutritious
meals for housewives and workers. Surprisingly enough, the
art gallery—called the Butler Gallery after the Chicago business-
man who donated five thousand dollars towards its establishment—proved more popular, and was far better patronized,
than the kitchen! This was not due solely to the superior
aesthetic sensibilities of the neighbourhood; it owed something
also to peasant prejudices and unwillingness to adopt new
customs, however beneficial these might appear to be. More
immediately successful was a coffee house attached to the
gymnasium which was erected within the next two years, and
which became the greatest single attraction for the many
hundred members of the boys' clubs.

In 1892 the first public children's playground in Chicago was
laid out on the site of some demolished houses: the property of

a wealthy young man, William Kent, who was 'converted' by hearing a speech by Jane Addams on the sharing of opportunities. For fifteen years he paid all taxes on the land, which was administered by Hull House for ten years and then taken over by the City Playground Commission. This was only one example of the development from spontaneous, unorganized beginnings to acknowledged civic responsibility that characterized so many of the pioneer activities of Hull House: from reading party to branch library, from study group to university extension course, · from studio to public school art society. And lest it be thought that, in the desperate conditions of Ward nineteen, too much attention was being given to the 'frills' of living—though Jane Addams and her associates never regarded art as a 'frill'—it should also be added: from Kindergarten to Mary Crane Nursery, and from 'Jane Club' to women's labour union. The systematic investigations into local conditions carried out by Hull House workers were a natural outcome of their personal acquaintance with misery amongst members of the clubs and classes: an acquaintance which could never have been followed up without the mutual trust and confidence that was born of a friendly social relationship.

Almost in the first weeks of Hull House, an impromptu kindergarten was set up to accommodate the young children of the numerous working mothers in the area: children who previously had either roamed the streets unprotected all day, or remained locked up alone in their tenement rooms. The first three crippled children who came to the house were victims of this neglect:

. . . one had fallen out of a third-storey window, another had been burned, and the third had a curved spine due to the fact that for three years he had been tied all day long to the leg of the kitchen table, only released at noon by his older brother who hastily ran in from a neighboring factory to share his lunch with him. [10]

The nursery was maintained, at first in a back-street cottage and later in a specially-built Children's House, for sixteen years, after which it was adopted by the United Charities of Chicago. The Mary Crane Nursery, as it was then called, is

still accommodated at Hull House, but is now under the supervision of the National College of Education.

The founding of the Jane Club in 1891 formed the first vital
link in the chain of organized women's labour, as yet almost
unheard of in Chicago. Only one women's union then existed,
that of the skilled bookbinders. Most women were employed
in the clothing industry, under abominable 'sweat shop'
systems: either working at home in their overcrowded tenements or in unhygienic workshops with no control over hours
or conditions. The Jane Club was originally established for the
benefit of factory girls, who were unwilling to organize themselves for strike action for fear that they would lose their jobs
and be unable to pay for their lodgings. It was notable in
springing from an initiative taken by the girls themselves.
'Wouldn't it be fine', asked one of them, 'if we had a boarding
club of our own, and then we could stand by each other in a
time like this?'[11] The idea spread, apartments were rented near
Hull House, and in May 1891 fifteen young women moved in
to live together on a co-operative basis; after one month the
club was self-supporting and in three years time it had fifty
members: the first boarding-club of its kind in the United
States. In 1898 a new club house was built with a gift of 15,000
dollars from friends of Hull House.

Meanwhile, other groups were organizing themselves at Hull
House into the first women's labour unions on any large scale:
the shirtmakers and cloakmakers met there, and the Dorcas
Federal Labor Union was founded by one of the residents.
Jane Addams was elected vice-president of the National
Woman's Trade Union League in 1904. It was not for nothing
that she was to observe many years later:

Even in the very first years of Hull House we began to discover that
our activities were gradually extending from the settlement to a
participation in city and national undertakings.[12]

The primary impulse for any activity at Hull House was
always a response to human need, at whatever level it presented
itself: practical, moral, intellectual or aesthetic. All needs were
taken care of, and all were given their rightful due. Inevitably,
in the conditions of the neighbourhood, a great deal of effort

had to be expended on the alleviation of sheer, physical misery
of a kind that would never have been allowed to fester under a
properly-conducted civic administration. This did not deter the
residents; it was one of the reasons why they had come. The
victims of a college education became one with the victims of
under-privilege in such humble tasks as washing newborn
babies and laying-out the dead. On one occasion, Jane Addams
and Julia Lathrop successfully delivered an unmarried mother
of her baby while the Irish matrons of the block stood by and
refused to contaminate themselves with the 'stigma' of illegiti-
macy.

But was that really their job? Jane wondered: 'this doing
things that we don't know how to do'. To which 'J.L.' replied:
'If Hull House does not have its roots in human kindness it is
no good at all'.[13] This was sufficient answer for the moment.
But Jane Addams was soon to understand that mere 'kindness'
was not enough; and that this root, though vital, was only one
small member of the social tree. Nor was kindness in fact the
great leveller that was needed 'to add the social function to
democracy'. No charity worker could vie with the generosity
of the poor to each other, wrought as it was out of a common
experience of stark subsistence when the sharing of a last crust
might well be the only possible assurance of a crust in return at
the hour of need. She could, however, if she were willing to
progress beyond charity, discover and remove the causes of that
need. No amount of sympathy could close the gap with under-
privilege, because education always conferred a hidden ace: the
trick not only of knowing what was wrong, but of knowing
how to put it right. And here, in recognizing the responsibilities
of superior education, lay the great strength of the Hull House
team.

The achievements in social research of the first five years were
reviewed in *Hull House Maps and Papers*, published in 1895.
This was sub-titled: 'A presentation of nationalities and wages
in a congested district of Chicago', and consisted of articles by
Jane Addams and eight co-workers together with maps based
on information supplied by a resident worker to the United
States Bureau of Labor. This survey revealed that there were
no less than nineteen different nationalities represented in
Ward nineteen, and that the majority lived in conditions of

indescribable squalor. Greeks slaughtered sheep in their own
basements; Italian women sorted rags collected from city
dumps in courtyards swarming with children; bakers made
their bread in open spaces beneath the filthy pavements. These
were only a few of the damning facts uncovered by the Hull
House investigators and recorded in papers such as Florence
Kelley's 'The Sweating System'; 'The Chicago Ghetto', by
Charles Zeublin; 'The Bohemian People in Chicago', by
Josefa H. Zeman; and 'The Cook County Charities', by Julia
Lathrop. Ellen Starr contributed 'Art and Labor' and Jane
Addams herself wrote on 'The Settlement as a Factor in the
Labor Movement'.

Already, her thoughts were moving beyond the simple
impulse to create a 'cathedral of humanity' as a haven for the
under-privileged, in the direction of the hard facts of civic and
state legislation. In this paper was recorded in black and white
her conviction that 'the settlement is bound to pledge itself to
industrial organization'. This did not necessarily mean that
Jane Addams, and Hull House, were to throw themselves
uncritically on the side of the labour movement; but rather
that they must recognize the organization of labour as being
both necessary and right for the proper functioning of a
democratic society. Her own role she saw as a summons to both
capital and labour to work together in order to uphold the
unity of life: a unity that was larger than either side, but
required the participation of both. She quoted in this connection a saying of Mazzini: 'We have torn the great and
beautiful design of Democracy. Each party has snatched a rag
of it, and parades it as proudly as if it were the whole flag'.[14]

To uphold the unity of life meant also to uphold its diversity,
and nowhere was this doctrine better demonstrated than at
Hull House itself, where by this time upwards of forty varied
activities and associations were established. In addition to the
clubs already mentioned there were college extension courses;
summer schools; a students' association; the Paderewski club
for children; the Phalanx club for men; the 'eight-hour' club,
to encourage women to stand by an eight-hour day in factories;
the Working People's Social Science club; an Arnold Toynbee
club and a Lincoln club; a Chicago Question club; and the
Nineteenth Ward Improvement Club, leading to the creation

of a Civic Federation Ward Council. There was also a savings bank, cookery school, public dispensary and employment bureau; and the list of activities and services is still far from complete.

It may be judged even from these few examples out of five years of progress, that Hull House was from the outset a phenomenal success. There could be no doubt in Jane's mind, or anybody else's, that it was fulfilling a much-felt need. And until 1892, when industrial investigations began to threaten the local vested interests, the public reception of the phenomenon was almost wholly favourable—if at times a little puzzled. In its first year, no less than 50,000 people came to the House; by the second year, visitors averaged a steady 2,000 a week—and most of them were seen personally by Jane Addams. After five years, there were fifteen resident workers; at the end of a decade these had grown to twenty-five. Hull House was the first 'mixed' residential settlement in America, although for three years all the residents were women. Then some of the non-resident male helpers took an adjacent cottage on Polk Street, carrying on with their own jobs for the most part and assisting the settlement in their spare time. All work in the settlement was voluntary, and residents met their living expenses on a co-operative basis.

The personnel of these early years, as described by Linn in his biography, were a remarkably distinguished group, showing a rare diversity of talent. Ellen Starr, who had come to Hull House as an artist, became passionately involved in the organization of women's labour. Julia Lathrop, another first-year resident, was a trained investigator who rose to be head of the United States Children's Bureau. Of a different character was Florence Kelley, married and divorced, the mother of three children, a lawyer and a formidable fighter for women's and children's rights: after a period as factory inspector she organized the National Consumers' League, of which she was chief executive for thirty years. Another staunch ally, though never a resident, was Mrs Bowen, president of the Hull House Woman's Club for seventeen years, founder of the Chicago Juvenile Court and donor of the Bowen Country Club, as a memorial to her husband, for the recreation of Hull House members.

Then there was Alice Hamilton, doctor and scientist, who could bath an Italian baby or track down a typhus germ with the same compassionate efficiency that she brought to bear in maintaining Jane Addams' health; she was to become professor of pathology at the Women's Medical College of Northwestern University and later, professor of industrial medicine at Harvard. She remained one of Jane Addams' closest associates in all her undertakings. Many fine artists were attracted to the liberal atmosphere of Hull House, amongst them: Mrs Pelham, a former actress, and Edith de Nancrede of the little theatre; Norah Hamilton, who illustrated *Twenty Years at Hull House*; Enella Benedict directing the art studio and Eleanor Smith the music school. Resident men included the painters Carl Linden and Frank Hazenplug; Francis Hackett of the *Chicago Evening Post*; and a mysterious Mr Twose, amiably eccentric, who taught handicrafts and took five o'clock tea in the nude on summer afternoons—not, it should be added, in public.

One other woman should be mentioned, of no single outstanding accomplishment but of great importance in the life of Jane Addams. Mary Rozet Smith came to 'help' at Hull House at the age of twenty, and remained one of its most devoted supporters until her death forty-three years later. With family responsibilities, wealth, and no profession, she never became a resident but generally 'looked after things', especially things connected with children; and, with no particular qualifications, won friends and influence by her sheer sweetness of character. More than any other Hull House worker, says Linn, she understood the truth: 'it is more blessed to give than to receive'. More than any other, too, she won the affection of Jane Addams: it was for Mary Smith, after the death of her father, that she came nearest to an expression of personal love. It must surely have been an affinity not of the mind—there is no suggestion of equality here—but of temperament. Linn quotes a rather pathetic little poem to M.R.S.,[15] found among Jane Addams' papers, in which she speaks of 'delivering love'; delivering, that is, from the 'one absorbing care' of Hull House that had hitherto claimed all the attention not only of her brain but of her heart. The poem was written following an attack of typhoid fever in 1895. It seems to indicate that although the sorrow, sickness and frustration of Jane's early years had tended to diffuse her strong capacity for affection into a generalized compassion, there was still an unfulfilled need arising from her own deprivation of the closest bonds of family life: those bonds to which she attached such importance in the life of society could not have been unimportant to herself. Indeed, the paramountcy of 'affection' in human relationships was one of her recurring themes.

The first ten years at Hull House established the reputation of Jane Addams as a national figure. It was a reputation based not upon books—she had published none by the turn of the century—but upon the concrete example of her work. The settlement movement was spreading rapidly, both in her own city—notably in Dr Graham Taylor's 'Chicago Commons' and the university settlement of Mary McDowell—and far beyond. She was in continual demand as a speaker at summer schools and congresses, women's clubs and businessmen's luncheons, before legislative committees and labour unions. Many of her talks were later printed as magazine articles and, subsequently, incorporated in her books.

It may be opportune at this point to try and analyse the sources of her influence. Surrounded as she was by as brilliant a galaxy of women as were ever gathered under one roof, Jane Addams still, without conscious effort, shone supreme. Most of her co-workers were to achieve distinction in high public offices, but Jane remained all her life an inveterate amateur. The only paid post she ever held was as Ward Inspector of Streets and Alleyways. She had none of the stamp of the 'public woman'; she lacked the craggy feature, the flashing eye and the well-braced contour that makes for the successful executive of either sex. At twenty-nine, when Hull House was opened, she had still a soft and girlish look, withdrawn and a little blurred by diffidence. By the age of thirty-five, the blur was moulded into calmness; the eyes had steadied and brightened —not with a flash but a twinkle, although the twinkle never quite extinguished an underlying sadness. This rounded mould settled and in time expanded, but never perceptibly hardened. Jane Addams had the authority derived from wisdom rather than from power. As Linn commented, summing up the first ten years at Hull House:

She had given all her sympathy, all her time, all her energy, and most of her money; she had got an understanding which was at least as clear as that of anybody else in the field, and her 'field was the world'. So at least the philosophers seem to have thought, and the social workers, and the neighbors; and so the country at large apparently came to think, for on the popular conception of that understanding of hers is based her chief reputation as a great American. Her tolerance, her courage, her devotion, even her intelligence, kindly spoken of as they all have been from time to time, are incidental to this understanding that she got from living at Hull House. If her understanding was wrong, she misled hundreds of thousands; if her understanding was wrong, her influence was really unfortunate, 'a menace' as some have called it. [16]

Here is the whole crux of Jane Addams' influence, and her significance for our time as well as her own. It is on the rightness of her understanding far more than on her specific achievements in local, national or international affairs, that her claim to greatness as well as goodness must stand or fall. But, in 1899, the understanding had not yet worked out to its fullest extent. Hull House was built in a city, and the city was impinging on the house; as the state was to impinge on the city; and, ultimately, the world on the state.

NOTES

[1] *Twenty Years at Hull House*, p. 92.
[2] *Ibid.*, pp. 97-8.
[3] *Ibid.*, pp. 98-9.
[4] *Ibid.*, p. 111.
[5] *Ibid.*, pp. 120-1.
[6] *Ibid.*, p. 116.
[7] *Ibid.*, p. 117.
[8] *Ibid.*, p. 124.
[9] *Ibid.*, p. 127.
[10] *Ibid.*, p. 168.
[11] *Ibid.*, p. 136.
[12] *My Friend, Julia Lathrop* (New York, Macmillan, 1935), p. 74.
[13] *Ibid.*, p. 53.
[14] 'The Settlement as a Factor in the Labor Movement', *Hull House Maps and Papers* (New York, Crowell, 1895), p. 200.
[15] *Jane Addams*, by J. W. Linn, p. 289.
[16] *Ibid.*, p. 193.

Chapter 5

THE FAIR CITY

IN 1889 when Jane Addams came to Chicago it could fairly be described as a city of garbage, graft and gangsters. Crime flourished with the connivance of the police. Public offices, as well as votes, were openly bought and sold. Politicians operated their own private rackets in gambling, drink and prostitution. Epidemics swept through the slums unchecked by any laws of hygiene. In 1894 the Civic Federation estimated that out of the city's sixty-eight aldermen, fifty-seven were 'grafters'.

That same year the British correspondent W. T. Stead wrote his famous indictment, 'If Christ Came to Chicago'[1]: 'What would he discover?' asked Stead. 'Vice, criminality, corruption and above all neglect, such as no other late nineteenth-century city would tolerate'.

Six years later the position had not materially improved, and the American reporter Lincoln Steffens could write:

It is first in violence, deepest in dirt; loud, lawless, unlovely, ill-smelling, new . . . Criminally it was wide open, commercially it was brazen, and socially it was thoughtless and raw . . . everybody was for himself and none was for Chicago.[2]

To such unpromising material Jane Addams applied the search for 'a new social ethic for the industrial age' which was the main focus of her creative thinking during the first twenty years at Hull House; as, similarly, a quarter of a century after her, Albert Schweitzer was to take his search for an ethic of civilization to the heart of primeval Africa. The fruits of Jane Addams' thinking are preserved in her autobiography of that period, *Twenty Years at Hull House* (1910); in the poignantly imaginative *Spirit of Youth and the City Streets* (1909); in the wide intellectual sweep of *Newer Ideals of Peace* (1907); and, with greatest concentration, in the powerfully incisive *Democracy and Social Ethics*, a book that is hardly less challenging today than when it was published in 1902.

Democracy and Social Ethics is clearly authoritative even though written by a woman—and one with no formal training in political or social theory; to this fact, no dount, may be attributed its orginality and freshness, growing as it did out of first-hand experience. It is in no sense a 'handbook', although it is certainly a 'guide'—but for statesmen and philosophers rather than for workers in the field. For it is a record not merely of experience, but of experience filtered through the judgment of a first-class mind, and thereby gaining the stamp both of permanence and universality. The material is compiled from twelve lectures given in colleges and university extension courses over the preceding ten years, and ranges from a precise dissection of the anatomy of charity to a charter for industrial amelioration and political reform. More than any other of her books, it demonstrates the Hull House 'method' that was so largely evolved out of the personality of one woman, its founder; and one, curiously enough, who could scarcely have been less addicted to the 'cult of the personality'.

Proceeding always 'from the concrete to the abstract'—and then, it might be added, back again to the individual, human person as a test of the fitness of the abstract principle—Hull House participation in civic, state, national and, ultimately, international organizations, progressed broadly from charity operated by voluntary agencies to welfare underwritten by legislation; from philanthropy operated by enlightened capitalism to industrial democracy underwritten by labour unions. This was, at least in Jane Addams' view, an inescapable development. What was wrong with charity? What was wrong with philanthropy? Both, she argued, were inadequate to an age that demanded for its orderly progress a social rather than an individual morality. And, sometimes, they were not even moral at the individual level. The charity-worker was dishonest in her assumption of a superiority that was based only on status; and, compared to the industrial worker, a 'parasitic' status at that. The philanthropist was self-deceiving if he imagined his generosity to be wholly disinterested, whilst at the same time he denied his workers their natural right to the 'associated effort' that would make his bounty superfluous.

Similarly, although corruption might be cheaper than taxation —and sometimes, through a composite of bribery and what Jane Addams called 'the stalking survival of village kindness' to the widow and the orphan, did confer short-term benefits on the very poor—it was not a tolerable alternative to an efficient and honest administration. And it was clear that, in order to achieve the latter, the former would have to go. Hull House fought two campaigns against the re-election of the notorious Alderman Powers who was alleged to have 'paved the ward with ten-dollar bills'; both were unsuccessful. The power of popular sentiment, which Jane Addams never under-estimated, was still too great; and it could often be a barrier to reform. She recalls in this connection an early 'blunder' of Hull House in proposing that an orphan child who had died should be buried at public expense, and the storm of protest this evoked from the local women who insisted on collecting amongst themselves to give the mite decent burial. How then could reactionary sentiment, so often adhering from the best of motives to inappropriate or obsolete ends, be geared to social progress? She attempted to find an answer in a paper called *Ethical Survivals in City Politics*[3], an excellent example of her insistence on the concrete case:

Ideas operate upon the popular mind only through will and character, and goodness has to be dramatized before it reaches the mass of men. Ethics and political opinions can come to the common people only through example—through a personality which seizes the imagination.

She was referring here to the hold which even a corrupt politician may have upon the people by the judicious dispensation of a few big-hearted gestures. But the supreme example of such a personality was, of course, her own.

For all these reasons, then—subjective and objective, personal and practical—the resources of Hull House were devoted, in its second phase, to the struggle for a better society; for the creation of that ideal city where, in Aristotle's phrase, 'men live a common life for noble ends'. But the common life—the concrete situation—must come first. There could be no striving for noble ends if the everyday means were lacking to the fulfilment of those universal human needs without which moral aspiration was both a mockery and a chimera: family affection, social security, co-operation in labour, and re-creative leisure. All these, Hull House had sought to establish within its own bounds; and now, if any permanent gain was to be made, the bounds must be extended: the spontaneous ethical impulse must be harnessed to appropriate institutions.

The success of this effort may be judged by the long-term achievement of replacing a sporadic, often chaotic, voluntary activity for the relief of direst need by established, public services on behalf of all citizens. Charitable effort in Chicago had never been co-ordinated until a Bureau of Organized Charities was set up under the supervision of a Hull House resident to cope with the appalling distress in the winter of financial depression following the World's Fair. At the same time, a group of citizens formed the Civic Federation, but Jane Addams resigned from its street cleaning committee when she realized that to reduce unemployment by providing cut-price labour was no real service to the worker. In 1893 Julia Lathrop was appointed to the Illinois State Board of Charities, but resigned in 1901 because of political corruption in the organization; she rejoined the board in 1905. Jane Addams was appointed first woman president of the National Conference of Charities and Corrections, a body of more than thirty years' standing, in 1909. Her presidential address to the 1910 conference in St Louis, on 'Charity and Social Justice', broke new ground in bringing the conference to a consideration of the economic causes of low industrial standards; a development that was to have wide political repercussions within the next two years. In 1908 she was one of the founders of the Chicago School of Civics and Philanthropy, which ultimately became the School of Social Service Administration of Chicago University; and it was perhaps no coincidence that Chicago had been the first American university to open a department of sociology in 1892.

Meanwhile, practical measures initiated at Hull House for the improvement of health and housing were rapidly being consolidated. The Nineteenth Ward Improvement Association had made a start by tackling the inadequate paving and refuse disposal in the ward: on one occasion Jane herself had shovelled off the top eight inches of the foot and a half of refuse that carpeted the street. This was during her tenure of office as 'garbage inspector' to which she was appointed by the mayor in 1895 at a salary of a thousand dollars a year, after she had made a bid for the contract for refuse disposal in the ward. It was not a popular appointment with Alderman Powers and his friends, who accused her of neglect of her duties—the job was no sinecure, and involved rising at six o'clock to supervise the men starting work, bullying the contractor for an adequate number of carts, and bringing defaulters to court—and she eventually paid over her salary to a deputy from Hull House. This arrangement was continued for three years, and the office was incorporated in the civil service—until Alderman Powers abolished it, substituted a 'ward superintendent', and made the job eligible only to men!

Disease and bad housing oppressed the neighbourhood with a double yoke that could only be lifted in unison; and lifted it was, with the lever of Hull House research. The ward's mortality rate fell by 1898 from third to seventh in the city. Through the agency of the City Homes Association, a model Tenement House Ordinance was passed in 1901. The three basement bath-tubs at Hull House, thrown open to the neighbourhood, made the case for a Public Bath-house. Following a typhoid epidemic in 1902—one of several, Jane Addams herself having suffered severely from the disease in 1895—residents traced the cause to the plumbing in adjacent houses; this survey caused Dr Alice Hamilton to make a thorough bacteriological study which led to the dismissal for incompetence of eleven out of twenty-four employees of the Sanitary Bureau. Other investigations dealt with milk supplies, midwifery and narcotics; the last resulting in a new law regulating the sale of cocaine in 1907. Dr Hamilton later carried out research for the Commission on Occupational Diseases which the Governor of Illinois appointed in 1910.

Above all, it was through their work for children that the Hull House pioneers staked their claim on posterity. Since the earliest resident workers were all women, it was natural that the condition of juveniles should have been one of their prior concerns; for Jane Addams, the most deeply-felt concern of all.

Her visions of the fair city, the democratic society and the peaceful world were alike dedicated to the service of youth. Her own favourite amongst her books was *The Spirit of Youth and the City Streets*: a little masterpiece of the compassionate imagination, playing on the grimmest aspects of industrial life and illuminating them with wonder and hope. In the eternally-renewed spirit of youth, she believed, lay not only the hope but the possibility of that new human consciousness that would one day illuminate the life of man. As in the Chicago of 1900, so in London and New York and Moscow the same spirit still walks; and the same crowds jostle it off the pavement with power-blinded eyes:

It is as if we ignored a wistful, over-confident creature, who walked through our city streets calling out 'I am the spirit of Youth! With me, all things are possible!' We fail to understand when he wants or even to see his doings, although his acts are pregnant with meaning, and we may either translate them into a sordid chronicle of petty vice or turn them into a solemn school for civic righteousness.

We may either smother the divine fire of youth or we may feed it. We may either stand stupidly staring as it sinks into a murky fire of crime and flares into the intermittent blaze of folly or we may tend it into a lambent flame with power to make clean and bright our dingy city streets. [4]

The Chicago streets of the 1890s told their own 'sordid chronicle', too obvious to need translation.

The first steps towards a more humane treatment of 'juvenile delinquents' in Illinois were taken by the liberal Governor Altgeld, who in *Our Penal Machinery and its Victims* (1884) had pointed out that approximately one third of all young people arrested as 'first offenders' were subsequently found to be innocent: and in 1882, the number of juveniles arrested in the city of Chicago was 32,800! In 1908, the number had dropped to 15,000; but still practically the whole machinery of the criminal courts was geared to the age group 13-25.

The need for a separate court to deal with juvenile offenders was pressed by Mrs Lucy Flower, chairman of the department of Philanthropy of the Civic Federation, with the backing of Julia Lathrop and Jane Addams. And when the Juvenile Court —the first in the world—was established by law in 1899 Julia

Lathrop was chairman of its committee, to be followed by another Hull House worker, Mrs Bowen. The probation service —on which the successful functioning of a juvenile court almost entirely depends—also sprang from the pioneer work of a Hull House resident, Mrs Stevens, who had for several years been in the habit of attending the nearest police station and taking unofficial charge of all juveniles arrested for minor offences. She was appointed first probation officer to the Court in 1899, and at the time of her death in 1900 was head of a team of six.

When the Court acquired its own model building, together with a detention centre, in 1907, the committee organized the Juvenile Protective Association which met weekly—and still meets—at Hull House. Disputing the common assumption that 'the craving for pleasure must be ministered to only by the sordid', as Jane Addams put it, the Association was successful in pressing for the opening of social centres, recreation rooms, public gardens and lakeside bathing beaches. In addition, a medical clinic and psychopathic institute were established at the Court; the latter, also the first of its kind, was after five years taken over by the county authorities and later developed into the state Institute for Juvenile Research.

An intensive study of truancy by a Hull House resident had early shown the relation of this misdemeanour with subsequent delinquency; and the causes of truancy were seen to lie not only in bad social conditions but also in the inadequacies of the educational system. In 1905 Jane Addams became a member of the Chicago Board of Education and she soon discovered, through disputes between the Board and the Teachers' Federation, that there could be no hope of improving the content of education until the administration of the public school system was freed from political exploitation:

In every city for many years the politician had secured positions for his friends as teachers and janitors; he had received a rake-off in the contract for every new building or coal supply or adoption of school books. [5]

To remedy this, the Board had appointed an independent Superintendent of schools with overall control—and thereby ran into trouble with the teachers who resented this 'dictation'

E

by the administration, which fixed not only salaries but curri-
cula. They were, indeed, caught between the Scylla of corruption and the Charybdis of authoritarian rule; and Jane
Addams, seeing right as well as wrong on both sides, could do
nothing to rescue them, although for two years she was Chairman of the School Management Committee. Her membership
of the Board was terminated in 1909 and not renewed; her own
contribution, she felt, had been 'inglorious'. She had succeeded
in alienating both sides: the Teachers' Federation accused her
of selling out to business interests in the administration; and
the business men dismissed her as a mere visionary. It was one
of her rare failures in mediation, due to a misunderstanding of
her aims: unlike the other parties, she was concerned not with
the advancement of certain interests but with the advancement
of education. And in fact, says Linn, 'she did as much as anyone
to promote in Chicago the recreational principle in public
school education'. She also wrested out of defeat a characteristic
conclusion:

Before my School Board experience, I thought that life had taught
me at least one hard-earned lesson, that existing arrangements and
the hoped for improvements must be mediated and reconciled to
each other, that the new must be dovetailed into the old as it were,
if it were to endure; but on the School Board I discerned that all
such efforts were looked upon as compromising and unworthy, by
both partisans. [6]

Nevertheless, her principle that 'the new must be dovetailed
into the old', was vindicated in yet another struggle: the
campaign for labour legislation. Thanks to investigations in-
stigated by Mrs Florence Kelley for the Illinois State Bureau of
Labor, and with the support of Governor Altgeld, the first
factory law of Illinois was passed in 1893: this fixed a minimum
age of fourteen for juvenile workers and an eight-hour day for
women in factories and workshops. The only child labour laws
previously in existence were confined to coal-mining. It was
not uncommon in Chicago for children of as little as four or
five years old to be pressed into service to pull threads, hour
after weary hour, for their mothers' sweat-shop sewing. When
only a little older, they would be sent out to factory-work

under abominable, and sometimes dangerous, conditions. Several Hull House boys were injured, and one was killed, for lack of a safety-guard on the machine at which they worked; the owners took no action. Little girls at the Christmas party refused sweets because they worked in a candy factory and 'couldn't bear the sight of it'. A girl of twelve was the highest wage-earner in one Italian family—until she died of overstrain. Another girl, Russian Jewish, committed suicide because she dared not forfeit a week's wages in order to repay a debt. But a year later the eight-hour clause was repealed as 'unconstitutional'; and Mrs Kelley's appointment as first factory inspector was terminated in two years. It was not until 1903 that adequate child labour laws were enforced in Illinois, and Jane Addams came to regard the 1893 law as a 'premature' measure that, even though legally enacted, was doomed to failure because of inadequate preparation and lack of the will to enforce it.

This was not surprising in the condition of bitter labour relations which existed at that time. From about 1880 Chicago had suffered a series of strikes that came to a head in the violent 'Haymarket Riot' of 1886, when bombs were thrown and the anarchists who were alleged to have incited the action were hanged. Indeed, 'anarchists'—a term of abuse that was frequently extended to any 'radical' or 'agitator'—enjoyed the status of tribal devils that has since passed to 'communists', and with an equally broad interpretation. In pardoning three anarchists after the passing of this first factory act, it was said that Governor Altgeld signed his own political death warrant; although it took another three years to get him out of office. In those three years, 'Viper' Altgeld—as he was known to readers of the virulent *Chicago Tribune*—found his chief henchmen (and women) in the workers of Hull House. At his funeral in 1902 the only speakers were his law-partner Clarence Darrow, the Reverend Frank Crane—and Jane Addams. It was little wonder that Hull House was becoming known as a 'nest of radicals' and that in the view of some citizens Jane Addams ought to be 'hanged to the nearest lamp-post'. [7]

Hull House was already under suspicion for its sponsoring of the Working People's Social Science Club. This had been founded in 1890 by an Englishman, and was to meet regularly every Wednesday evening for seven years. Here members of all

shades of opinion—including anarchists, radicals and socialists
—were permitted to give free vent to their fervour: a rare
opportunity in those days when feeling was running at fever
pitch, but with no organized channels for its expression and no
social data by which to measure its accuracy. Hull House
provided both data and facilities for expression, adding to these
a third benefit: the means for a constructive application of
knowledge and opinion in social action. To do this did not
imply the endorsement of any or all of the participating schools
of thought. Jane Addams insisted again and again, and was to
reiterate at the conclusion of *Twenty Years at Hull House*, that
in its pursuit of the civic ideal 'the Settlement cannot limit its
friends to any one political party or economic school'.

Jane Addams only once took part in a campaign on behalf of
a political party, and this was in support of Theodore Roosevelt's newly-formed Progressive Party in 1912. The campaign
had in effect begun in 1909 when the Conference of Charities
and Corrections, besides electing Jane as its national president,
set up a Committee on Occupational Standards to undertake
a three-years' survey of industrial conditions. Its report, with
recommendations for minimum standards, was adopted at the
1912 Conference with the support of twenty national organizations; and further, was presented by a group of social workers
to Colonel Roosevelt, who promptly incorporated its proposals
into his party platform. It was for this reason that Jane Addams
found herself one of the chief speakers at the Progressive Party
convention in Chicago that August. As she explained it herself:

I was there . . . because the platform expressed the social hopes
so long ignored by the politicians . . . because the very sentiments
of compassion and desire for social justice were futile unless they
could at last find expression as an integral part of corporate government. [8]

She canvassed this cause as a campaign speaker across North
and South Dakota, Iowa, Nebraska, Oklahoma, Colorado
and Missouri, and her advocacy—herself voteless—was said
to have brought Roosevelt a million votes. Nevertheless, he was
roundly beaten at the polls; and she was forced to recognize
that this campaign, too, was ill-timed and out of touch with

popular sentiment. But she did not feel that it was wasted, because 'new parties ultimately write the platforms for all parties', paving the way for existing organizations—to whom direct appeal had been fruitless—to take up the desired cause. Party politics, however, were not really Jane Addams' *forte*; and she was to give her support thereafter, not on a party basis but for men and policies on their merits: Wilson (Democrat) in 1916; Debs (Socialist) in 1920; La Follette (Progressive) in 1924; Hoover (Republican) in 1928 and 1932.

Where politics had failed, could organized labour succeed in establishing the good society? It could at least redress the balance of an uneven-handed justice, and it was in this sense that Hull House was committed to support of the labour movement. The weak must be defended—because they were weak, and therefore ill-used. But this did not mean that the 'under-dog' was always and infallibly right: on the contrary, 'very often he is but obscurely right, sometimes only partially right, and often quite wrong'. [9] In a paper on 'Trades Unions and Public Duty' Jane Addams strongly defended the aims of the movement:

For many years I have been impressed with the noble purposes of trades-unions, and the desirability of the ends which they seek; and at the same time I have been amazed at the harshness with which their failures are judged by the public, and the undue stress which is laid upon the violence and disorder which sometimes accompany their efforts. [10]

Disorders arose, she suggested, through the failure of public opinion to realize that only the state itself could achieve these ends *without* disorder; the responsibility lay on the whole community, not on any one section of it. Similarly, although a strike might sometimes be necessary as the only available means of calling attention to an injustice, a just solution would not be achieved unless the unions on their side respected the principle of arbitration. Here was another demonstration of the need for a new social ethic, superseding the interests not only of the individual but of the sectional group: each group had a rightful place, but the parts must be subordinated to the whole in whatever social unit their interests co-existed.

Jane Addams had been made secretary of the Civic Federation's Industrial Arbitration Committee in 1893, and after the failure of arbitration in the Pullman Strike the following year, a campaign was started for the creation of a State Board of Conciliation and Arbitration. This was set up, but again the law proved in practice to be one of form rather than substance. Although arbitration was finally accepted in a garment workers' strike of 1896, it did not solve the causes of this and subsequent disputes. It was not until 1910 that Jane Addams achieved a significant triumph of arbitration in a textile strike involving 40,000 workers, spreading to 90,000. She refused to sign an agreement—although the international president of the garment workers' union had been willing to accept it—that did not include the right of collective bargaining; for without this right, she maintained, there would be a continual recurrence of labour troubles. This judgement was vindicated many years later by Sidney Hillman, President of the Amalgamated Clothing Workers' Union, who at a dinner in her honour in 1935 commented that the 1910 agreement had laid the foundation for industrial peace for over one hundred thousand workers in the industry.

But it was through the Pullman Strike of 1894 that Jane Addams achieved a more immediate fame: not as an arbitrator, for she was called away at the height of the dispute by the death of her eldest sister Mary and when she returned it was to find federal troops encamped on Halsted Street. Sympathies at Hull House had been divided, maintaining open contacts with both sides, and once again it was noted that this impartiality led only to a realization of the extreme bitterness and division 'along class lines'. The dispute was not in this case a simple issue of right and wrong. The Pullman workers had struck for a principle: the rights of organized labour against the personal whim of an autocratic, if benevolent, employer; a situation that time and patience might have amicably solved. The employer, George M. Pullman, was a noted philanthropist who had built a model town for his workers, and he was regarded by Jane Addams not as a capitalist bogeyman but as a figure of tragedy: the tragedy of maladjustment to changing conditions. It was his obstinate denial that there was any issue to arbitrate that led to the calling out of the railway workers in sympathy. Threatened with a general stoppage, the government intervened and the Pullman workers went back, beaten, with none of their legitimate grievances redressed.

But out of the strike came one contribution to industrial conciliation in the shape of a paper by Jane Addams, originally given before the Chicago Woman's Club and later printed[11], which she called 'A Modern Lear'. The Lear in this case was, of course, Pullman, and the whole complex analogy of conflicting wills and temperaments that may operate no less disastrously in social as in family relationships, is beautifully balanced and analysed. It is a notable addition to the social thinking of any age, and perhaps more than any other single achievement it established the reputation of Jane Addams as a national figure. It was a triumph of understanding over confused thinking, of imaginative insight over reckless action. The disaster must be viewed, she considered not only in its legal and sociological aspects but from 'those deep human motives which . . . determine events'. For Pullman, the very consciousness that he was a 'benefactor' prohibited the possibility of any equal human relationship with his men. Whilst for the workers on their side, emancipation must be generous enough to include the employer if it were not to result in a state comparable to that of Lear's unregenerate daughters: 'it is ours not yours'. The crux of the *impasse*, she saw, was the divergence of individual and social aims in an industry that had developed not by corporate effort but by 'the dictates of the capitalist'.

How then were the aims of the individual to be reconciled with those of society? Not, in Jane Addams' view, by the substitution of workers' for capitalist control: both concepts were based on an unreal view of human nature, and were therefore impracticable—for trade unionists could be no less corrupt than aldermen, as the 'phoney' teamsters' strike of 1905 flagrantly demonstrated. It was here that she differed from the orthodox socialists. Whilst accepting most of the practical implications of socialism she rejected its dogma outright, as she made clear in *Newer Ideals of Peace*. Since she was subjected to considerable misrepresentation on this issue, from both Right and Left, the relevant passage is worth quoting in full:

While the State spends millions of dollars and employs thousands of servants to nurture and heal the sick and defective, it steadfastly refuses to extend its kindliness to the normal working man. The Socialists alone constantly appeal for this extension. They refuse, however, to deal with the present State and constantly take refuge in the formulae of a new scholasticism. Their orators are busily engaged in establishing two substitutes for human nature which they call 'proletarian' and 'capitalist'. They ignore the fact that varying, imperfect human nature is incalculable, and that to eliminate its varied and constantly changing elements is to face all the mistakes and miscalculations which gathered around the 'fallen man' or the 'economic man' or any other of the fixed norms which have from time to time been substituted for expanding and developing human life. In time 'the proletarian' and 'the capitalist' will become the impedimenta which it will be necessary to clear away in order to make room for the mass of living and breathing citizens with whom self-government must eventually deal.[12]

Today, fifty years later, the 'impedimenta' are still with us. Already, at the beginning of the century, Jane Addams was looking beyond sectarianism towards the more potent ideal of a self-governing democracy.

But democracy could not be built in a day. Like her almost exact contemporaries in England, Beatrice and Sidney Webb, she believed firmly in 'the inevitability of gradualism'. As she was to put it in a paper at the National Conference of Social Work (which grew out of the old Conference of Charities and Corrections) in 1930:

the hoary abominations of society can only be done away by the steady impinging of fact on fact, of interest on interest, of will on will.

She closely resembled the Webbs, too, in her acceptance of the method of 'social engineering' and the high priority that municipal action must take, and she praised their 'brilliant' minority report of the Poor Law Commission on unemployment in 1909. But she would never have followed them in their later adulation of the Soviet-style, centralized administration, and in human sympathies they were worlds apart. The Webbs visited Hull House in 1893, and the incompatibility of the two women is aptly illustrated in the story of Jane accepting a cigarette from

Beatrice—with disastrous effects. It was the first one, and the only one, she ever smoked.

For Chicago, in the years before the first world war, the first step in the creation of a self-governing democracy was the elimination of corruption; the second was the establishment of an efficient and humane municipal government; the third, the absorption of the immigrant populations and the demonstration of one law for all citizens regardless of racial origin or creed; and the fourth, education for citizenship in a cosmopolitan, industrial society. These were not necessarily steps to be taken chronologically; they were so inter-related that an advance or a setback in one assisted or retarded the progress of all. In achieving the first and second steps it can be assumed that all forward-looking citizens were united; and it was rather in the third and fourth that the unique contribution of Hull House was most apparent. Its role in providing a haven for the newly-arrived immigrant is implicit in the whole philosophy of the settlement; but, if the haven was to become more than just a half-way house to full integration, this impulse too must be given institutional status. An appropriate form was found in the Immigrants' Protective League—how appropriate, may be judged by the fact that the League still functions from Hull House, although its clients today are Puerto Ricans and Mexicans rather than Italians or Greeks. Its first superintendent was Edith Abbott, and amongst early activities was an investigation into employment agencies that led to a bill providing for state-licensed, free employment bureaux in 1899. Some years later, during an anarchist scare following the assassination of President McKinley, the League organized a campaign against the extradition of Russian-born revolutionists: a stand that was upheld by Washington against the state's decision to return several thousand refugees to the Czarist regime. The only cure for attempted violence against authority, Jane Addams considered, was the extension of mutual rights and securities so as to include 'the veriest outcast' in the normal fellowship of society.

The immigrant peoples were an important influence, too, in her vision of an educated democracy that might form the microcosm for a genuine 'world community'. The vision found

one embodiment in the creation of the Hull House Labor
Museum. Starting from the simple desire to preserve and
encourage the varied skills of peasant craftsmen, as a means
of bridging the division not only between immigrants and their
new country but between the older immigrants and their
rapidly-Americanized children, the museum developed into an
extensive exhibition of industrial history, with its own trade
schools and workshops. This was one means of making a
'living connection' between the worker and his job which Jane
Addams felt was of such vital importance in establishing
industrial democracy: the connection, for instance, of primitive
spinning and weaving to the textile industry and to the classes
in embroidery, dress-making and basket-work conducted at
Hull House itself; or through the development of pottery, metal
and woodworking processes; or by the application of steam
power. Viewed in this perspective, the machine became not the
master but the tool of man's ingenuity.

The museum served also, in its training schools, to counteract
the destroying power of factory work for young people. The
inhibition of all imaginative, emotional, and indeed natural
motor impulses in adolescents by monotonous labour was,
Jane Addams believed, the greatest factor contributing to
juvenile delinquency; a 'delinquency' that was frequently no
more than the instinctive playing-out of ancestral skills inherited from the hunt for food or a mate. But if these skills
could be utilized in industry, through the application of
arts and crafts to commercial production for everyday use,
the quality of urban living could be transformed. Even by the
beginning of the present century, she considered, applied
science in industry had reached its limit in the development of
the machine: 'industrial advance will lie not in the direction
of improvement in machinery, but in the recovery and education of the workman'.[13]

The working-man must be taught the social and industrial
value of his labour; and in this respect, she considered, the
settlement had failed in its educational programme, which
scarcely touched the great mass of factory workers. The artist,
too, had failed in not bringing his insight to bear on this
problem; and Jane Addams went so far as to speak of 'the

solace of collective art' as a means of providing the workman with a human significance. [14]

The humanizing of industry, then, must go hand in hand with the humanizing of justice and the humanizing of government in order that the good life might be extended to the whole of society. Thanks to the Hull House reformers and their associates, by the end of their second decade this necessity was generally recognized; although Jane Addams added the characteristic rider that 'unless all men and all classes *contribute* to a good, we cannot be sure that it is worth having'. [15] It was still only imperfectly recognized, however, that the city-state—and, indeed, the nation-state—could no longer maintain its autonomy in a world whose problems were even then presenting themselves in economic rather than political terms. Whilst the United States government made knowledge of the Constitution its chief test of citizenship, Jane Addams observed in 1907, 'the real issues are being settled by the great industrial and commercial interests which are at once the products and the masters of our contemporary life'. [16] Supra-civic co-operation was already a reality in the inter-state commerce laws that regulated labour conditions and industrial diseases. This co-operation was extended internationally in the campaign against 'phossy jaw', to which the United States adhered in 1912. Jane Addams' early acquaintance with this disability in the London match-girls was to be renewed many years later in a Peking match factory where she was shown the last case of phossy jaw in the world, 'for its possibility had been outlawed throughout civilization'; [17] as a longstanding Vice-President of the American Association for Labor Legislation, she could claim some share in this progress. But perhaps the development that brought most rejoicing at Hull House was the foundation in 1912 of the Federal Children's Bureau for the protection of juveniles: although the idea had originated from a New York settlement, its first chief was Julia Lathrop; and its second, Grace Abbott (sister of Edith Abbott of the Immigrants' Protective League, of which she too had been Superintendent).

So, in a mood of hopeful achievement, ended the first twenty years at Hull House. The individual, ethical impulse of a small-town miller's daughter had started a chain-reaction that spread from neighbourhood to city; from municipality to state; from state to federation; and which still had not reached its limit. If the embryo of world consciousness was already conceived, it was to lie dormant in the womb of the subconscious for another thirty years. Other, more violent, forces were now assembled to burst through the carefully-constructed dams of eighteenth and nineteenth century rationalism. As the old ideals crumbled and were swept away, what new tide was rising to fill their place?

NOTES

1 Quoted by Linn in *Jane Addams*, p. 188.
2 *The Shame of Cities*, by Lincoln Steffens (Smith, 1904, reprinted from McClure's Magazine).
3 Quoted by Linn in *Jane Addams*, pp. 171-2.
4 *Spirit of Youth and the City Streets* (New York, Macmillan, 1909), pp. 161-2.
5 *Twenty Years at Hull House*, p. 333.
6 *Ibid.*, p. 336.
7 *Jane Addams*, by J. W. Linn, p. 157.
8 *Second Twenty Years at Hull House* (New York, Macmillan, 1930), p. 31.
9 *Ibid.*, p. 422.
10 *Journal of Sociology* (University of Chicago), Jan. 1899.
11 Printed in *The Survey* magazine of Chicago and included in *Satellite Cities*, by Graham R. Taylor (1915).
12 *Newer Ideals of Peace* (New York, Macmillan, 1907), p. 86.
13 *Spirit of Youth and the City Streets*, p. 131.
14 *Democracy and Social Ethics*, p. 219.
15 *Ibid.*, p. 220.
16 *Newer Ideals of Peace*, p. 42.
17 *Second Twenty Years at Hull House*, p. 21.

Chapter 6

DEATH OF AN IDEAL

JANE Addams was four and a half years old at the time of
Lincoln's death. She had imbibed with her mother's milk the
ideals of the American civil war. A roll of honour of the Addams
Guard, raised by her father, was mounted with full insignia
in the family living room. And one of her most vivid childhood
memories was of being driven by her father in the family
carriage—with her step-mother, step-brother and sister—to
visit the war eagle Old Abe at the state building in Wisconsin.
Here, the former emblem of the 8th Wisconsin regiment was
enjoying an honourable retirement after passing unscathed
through thirty-six skirmishes—or so the legend told.

For the youthful Jane it was a memorable journey,
epitomizing for her 'that search for the heroic and perfect
which so persistently haunts the young'; a search that, on this
occasion at least, was not in vain. Her inspiration was drawn,
however, less from the person of the ancient eagle, now in-
gloriously confined to a perch, than from the dome of the
Capitol itself, which seemed to encompass in its man-made
curve—prefiguring the 'cathedral of compassion' that was to
encompass all humanity—the surge of marching feet: 'of
soldiers marching to death for freedom's sake; of pioneers
streaming westward to establish self-government in yet another
sovereign state'. [1]

Her whole childhood, indeed, was bathed in a warm glow of
heroism, reflected in the spirit of brave men who had lost their
lives 'that the slaves might be free'. This was the moral currency
of her own time and place and she did not then doubt its
sterling value any more than her father, or Lincoln himself,
had done; given their situation, it was scarcely conceivable
that they could. And yet, the daughter of John Addams did
begin to question it; and grew up to repudiate utterly the old

morality of the righteous war in favour of the Christian doctrine of non-resistance. It was no simple rebellion of youth against the values of its elders. Jane Addams had always the greatest veneration for tradition, and she did not abandon lightly the orthodox patriotism of the Northern Union, or of the United States itself when the greater test of international conflict arose. She did not, in fact, ever 'repudiate' patriotism—any more than she had repudiated socialism—so much as see beyond it to a larger unity, as she constantly extended her vision to meet the challenge of change and growth.

Nor, unlike some pacifists, did she under-rate the heroic appeal of war and its hold upon the human spirit as a military motive at least as powerful as those of aggrandisement or oppression. The search for an alternative expression of heroism, for the 'moral equivalent' to war, was to occupy the second phase of her adult life as the search for a social ethic had occupied the first.

The two problems grew out of each other. It was perhaps significant for her philosophical development that, in Jane Addams' homeland of the Middle Western states, the soldier and the pioneer had seemed to march in step, so that militarism and government were inextricably linked. To establish 'law and order' was one thing; to build on this law and order a genuine 'social peace' was quite another, demanding new attitudes and new methods from both governors and governed. In *Newer Ideals of Peace* she spoke of the 'vestiges of militarism in city government', finding that these flourished most strongly in the police force; and she did not find it merely a coincidence that there too was the greatest corruption. But the military attitude was also apparent in the generally accepted concept of 'two nations', with its concern for the protection of property and the maintenance of the *status quo:*

The community is . . . divided into two camps, the repressed, who is dimly conscious that he has no adequate outlet for his normal life, and the repressive, represented by the cautious, careful citizen holding fast to his own—once more the conqueror and his humble people. [2]

In the strike method of the workers could be seen a logical

reaction to the authorized violence of the forces of repression. This attitude could only be changed by the development of new social forces at least as powerful as the old: and forces that, to be effective, must be rooted in 'impulses and experiences as primitive and profound as are those of struggle itself'. Always a realist, Jane Addams did not seek to deny or wish away the destructive, aggressive impulses; she saw rather that the strength of social morality lay in 'the irresistible coalescing of the altruistic and egoistic impulse'. And the agent to effect this coalescence, she discovered, was the principle of non-resistance! It was a principle, in Jane Addams' understanding, not of negative passivity but of an active dynamism charged with all the emotional force of 'virile goodwill'.

Her attachment to the doctrine of non-resistance had been formed probably in late adolescence, with roots both in primitive Christianity and in Tolstoyism. Her girlhood questionings of orthodox theology had led her back to the early Christians as the only true guardians of the faith: and the living truth that she perceived in the Christian martyrs was expressed less as a relation to God than as a relation to their Roman masters. She never had serious doubts about the validity of this truth, and she expressed her faith publicly as early as 1892:

The early Christians were pre-eminently non-resistant. They believed in love as a cosmic force . . . The spectacle of Christians loving all men was the most astounding Rome had ever seen. [3]

She was also practising it in her daily life at Hull House, as an incident during the visit of the Barnetts in 1891 reveals. Dame Henrietta Barnett, in her biography of her husband, described the tiresome habit of the small boys of Chicago, of ringing the doorbell at Hull House and then running away. As a good Christian citizen, she felt moved to reprimand them; but— rather to her bewilderment, one suspects—her intervention was not gratefully received:

On telling Miss Addams, her beautiful eyes filled with tears, and she said in her gentle, undulating American voice: 'You have put my work back, perhaps years. I was teaching them what is meant by "resist not evil".' [4]

A lot of fuss about a trifle, might well have been Mrs Barnett's private comment. But it was no small matter to Jane Addams, as the magnitude of her response demonstrated. 'Non-resistance', with its corollary of positive love, was the mainspring of her whole social philosophy. The term is misleading to modern ears, and its meaning is perhaps better expressed as 'non-violence', or *ahimsa* as Gandhi called it; in this sense, it is becoming widely recognized as an active social force. But in the nineteenth century, the corresponding influence was that of Tolstoyan non-resistance; and it was under this influence that Jane Addams expressed her philosophy.

She had begun reading Tolstoy at the age of twenty-one, and had gone on reading him with something of the awe of a disciple. But she was not uncritical of the master in his application of his doctrines. Her visit to him in 1896, when she received a somewhat dusty answer, did not reduce her to believing that the error was all on her side. Following a serious bout of typhoid fever, she was recuperating in Europe with Mary Smith, and the two women were escorted to the Count's home at Yasnaya Polyana by his British translator, Aylmer Maude.

The desire for a personal interview arose, on the part of Jane Addams, from a concern with the problem of poverty rather than with war and peace. It was the culmination of two years' anxious thought: how could one make 'living with the poor' a reality, and strip it of all pretence, except by sharing the lot of the neediest and humblest in the community? Tolstoy himself, in *What To Do?*—the outcome of a similar mental conflict—reached the conviction that there was no way of serving the peasant other than as a peasant, by assuming himself the burden of physical labour; and this he had undertaken to do. But, Jane now wanted to know, how had the doctrine worked out in practice? Had it resolved his doubts, and brought him the peace of fulfilment?

The meeting got off to a bad start, with Tolstoy commenting that there was enough material in one of her sleeves to make a child's smock. It was difficult to explain, in peasant Russia, that the sleeves of the average Chicago factory-girl were very much fuller than her own. But worse was to follow, with the exposure of Jane Addams as an 'absentee landlord' from the

Illinois farm that provided her with the necessities of life. The lesson was rubbed home by the timely appearance at the tea-table of Tolstoy's daughter, straight from a hard day's harvesting. Jane was impressed by this 'sermon of the deed', in which she saw that Tolstoy had been strongly influenced by the doctrine of 'bread labour' as expounded by the Russian peasant writer Timothy Bondaref. [5] But was this necessarily the only way, or the best way, for other countries to solve their economic problems? She retained her misgivings, and wondered whether Tolstoy might not be 'more logical than life'; and wondered also whether the payment of 'unrequited labour' was really an adequate settlement of life's complex debts.

Nevertheless, she resolved to test his theories for herself by undertaking at least two hours baking each morning at Hull House: an appropriate form of labour, she decided, for a miller's daughter who had acquired proficiency in bread-making at an early age. But on returning to Chicago, her resolution evaporated. To 'save her soul' by two hours' daily baking did not seem a good substitute for attending to the myriad human wants that perpetually clamoured to be met. She sought further guidance by visiting a Tolstoyan community in the Southern States; but again, although impressed by the power of conviction lived-out in action, she remained intellectually unconvinced. She saw a confusion of matter and spirit, and concluded that to test the things of the spirit too literally meant losing sight of the 'facts of life'.

She recorded some disappointment, too, with Tolstoy's interpretation of non-resistance, the application of which he seemed to limit to the use of physical force. Perhaps she had the example of his own family in mind when she commented that moral force, too, could be used equally ruthlessly 'to over-ride another's differences and scruples'. This was never her own method, and if her philosophy was less 'logical' than Tolstoy's it was more widely-inclusive; if her actions were sometimes inconsistent, the compromise was caused by generosity rather than meanness of spirit. As a delegate at the Progressive Party convention in 1912, she had voted for two battleships along with the programme of social reform; knowing, doubtless, that the battleships would be there under any government, but the reforms might not—and without reform, the battleships would

F

never go. Another example of her reluctance to use moral pressure in order to strike an advantageous bargain was recalled by Miss S. P. Breckinridge of the Chicago School of Social Service Administration, in connection with that same Progressive convention. [6] So anxious were the party organizers to obtain the *cachet* of Miss Addams' support, that she could have fixed her own terms for giving her assent. Many people hoped that she would make the condition that the party should advocate a policy of 'fair and equal treatment of the Negro', since its leaders were under a considerable influence from the Southern States. This she refused to do—not from any lack of sympathy with the cause of racial equality, for she had been a founder-member of the National Association for the Advancement of Coloured People in 1909 and she served on its national board until her death. It was simply, as Miss Breckinridge put it, that 'the use of force, whether physical, economical, or spiritual, was abhorrent to her'. One wonders whether Tolstoy would have approved of either of these apparent concessions of principle.

But in their admiration of the Russian peasant's tradition of 'passive resistance', and their hope that this example might lead the way to a new national policy of war-resistance by all peoples, Jane Addams and Tolstoy were one. It may be, too, that the impression she made on the master was less unfavourable than she supposed. For from the proceeds of *Resurrection*, which Tolstoy had published to aid the settlement of members of the Russian Dukhobor sect in Canada, of the five hundred dollars outstanding one half was given to Hull House. [7]

This was an acknowledgement, perhaps, of her fight for justice on behalf of immigrant anarchists and revolutionaries in the United States, most of whom were of Russian origin and many of whom were charged with crimes that were proved to be the work of *agents provocateurs* of the Czarist government. In this cause Jane Addams, and Hull House, suffered a good deal of persecution. Her efforts to obtain legal aid for the editor of an anarchist paper, who was arrested in the scare following President McKinley's assassination in 1901 by an avowed 'anarchist'—a Polish Jew—led to a bitter attack on her in the press and by correspondence from which the 'smear' was never quite obliterated. The attack was as illogical as it was

unjustified. Her sole purpose in advocating justice for the
immigrant was to uphold and strengthen the rule of law; it
in no sense implied approval of the methods of the revolutionists. She felt strongly, indeed, that violence in a just cause
was even more damaging than the violence of a reactionary
government, and at least as hard to forgive:

. . . when the sense of justice seeks to express itself quite outside
the regular channels of established government, it has set forth on a
dangerous journey inevitably ending in disaster, and this is true in
spite of the fact that the adventure may have been inspired by noble
motives. [8]

The statement is a model of constitutional propriety, that would
not have come amiss from a Conservative Prime Minister, and
it might easily lead the reader to a charge of reactionary rather
than over-radical sentiment. It was in fact a statement of belief
in the relation of ends and means; although radical ends
demanded radical means, the radical itself must be made
constitutional in order to become effective.

As with democracy, so with pacifism: a personal ethic was
not enough. It was necessary to establish the kind of institutions through which the ethic might achieve social reality; and
before it could achieve social reality, it must be made socially
acceptable. Through her experience with immigrant peoples of
many races, and through her efforts to establish a civilized
municipal administration, Jane Addams was convinced by the
beginning of the twentieth century that the 'war virtues' had
already outlived their usefulness and were only a deterrent to
further social advance. The old concept of the loyal citizen as
one who was 'ready to shed his blood for his country', was
both inadequate and obsolete. Aggression was finding its
contemporary outlet not in military adventure but in unrestricted commercial enterprise: the castle of the feudal war
lord was replaced by the factory of the business tycoon. Between
capital and labour, the normal relation was too often a state of
undeclared warfare that broke out periodically into open
conflict in the strike and the lock-out. In this situation, the way
forward must lie in the harnessing of industry as a whole to
the service of human need:

Under an enlightened industrialism, peace would no longer be an absence of war, but the unfolding of worldwide processes making for the nurture of human life. [9]

For the unfolding of these processes, the military ideals were useless; their realization demanded no less than the 'newer ideals' of peace. Peace, like democracy, must be released from the prison of abstract dogma and become a living force.

What was it that held men back from this next necessary stage in evolution? (Women were held back, she then believed, by the lack of a vote.) Social ideals were largely determined by the dominant schools of philosophy—which in turn were determined, at least in part, by prevailing social conditions— and philosophy was still dominated by the static ideals of the eighteenth century rationalists:

That old Frankenstein, the ideal man of the eighteenth century, is still haunting us, although he never existed save in the brain of the doctrinaire. [10]

This was strong language for Jane Addams, and intentionally so, for she saw that a false ideal was far more dangerous than no ideal at all and if persisted in—as the coming war was to demonstrate—might destroy the world. Already, the eighteenth century conception of 'unprogressive' human nature was refuted by nineteenth century evolutionism (as evolution in its turn was to be refuted by twentieth century fission); but the politicians, even by 1914, had not caught up.

Political democracy had been founded on the doctrine of the rights of man. But, said Jane Addams, human rights were not inborn or inalienable, and to enshrine them in a constitution did not guarantee their permanence. On the contrary, these rights must be won afresh by each generation in 'the tragic processes of experience'. The founders of American democracy, she maintained, had copied the European model too closely. In failing to take account of their own experience, they had blundered into the mistaken belief that 'if only the people had freedom, they would walk continuously in the paths of justice and righteousness'. [11] They had failed, in their political in-

stitutions, to provide any adequate vehicle for the expression
of popular will.

What was demanded by the 'new humanitarianism' of the
nineteenth century, Jane Addams believed, was that the
abstraction of 'humanity' must be broken down into its com-
ponent parts of men, women and children; the abstraction of
'democracy' must be submitted to the will of the people; the
abstraction of 'law and order' must give place to a fellowship
of common interest. Above all, the new humanitarianism must
be founded upon a 'cosmopolitan' ideal: even before the first
bugles of 1914 had sounded, scientific invention was demon-
strating that nationalism—for all practical if not for ideological
purposes—was already dead.

Dead, maybe—but unwilling to lie down. As the old jingles
sounded ever more stridently and out of tune, it was inevitable
that Jane Addams should be drawn into the organized peace
movement. Her biographer records that her first public ob-
objection to militarism was made in 1896 in connection with
the Hull House squad of 'Columbian Guards', a corps formed
during the World's Fair for the purpose of cleaning up the
city's streets. This admirable object was tarnished, in Jane's
eyes, by the desire of the boys to include military drill in their
training. A possible way out occurred to her: that the drill
should be conducted with sewer spades—which, she had noted,
'with their long narrow blades and shortened handles were not
so unlike bayoneted guns in size, weight and general appearance'. As long as she conducted the drill herself, the boys fell
in with this deception; but, once her personal exhortation was
withdrawn, they lapsed into self-consciousness and refused to
carry on. The experiment was not a success, but neither was it
a total failure: for this abortive beating of guns into sewer
spades was to be re-born in the 'pick and shovel peacemaking'
of the International Voluntary Service founded by Pierre
Ceresole in Switzerland after the first world war. But this
episode was not the end of military drill at Hull House, and in
1913 Jane Addams lifted her ban in deference to the deep
conviction of the Greek boys that it was their first duty to their
fatherland that they should train to fight the Turks. This was
another example of her sacrifice of a principle for the sake of a
concrete case:

With such a genuine motive at hand, it seemed mere affectation to deny the use of our boys' club building and gymnasium for organized drill.[12]

Greek youth, she observed in explanation, was still in the first stage of its inherited attitude towards the Turk.

But, however great the obstacles, it was imperative to press on to the next stage before the world was engulfed in hatred. From the Congress of Vienna in 1814 to the first World Court of Conciliation and Arbitration established at The Hague in 1899, plans had been instituted and conferences had been held, both in Europe and America, for the maintenance of international peace; and during this period, by mutual agreement of the 'concert of powers', major outbreaks of war had been avoided. Nevertheless, warlike acts, provocations and minor aggressions continued to threaten this precarious stability. In 1899 Jane Addams took an active part in a public campaign against the annexation of the Philippines by the United States. In 1912, her support for the Progressive Party was influenced not only by Theodore Roosevelt's social policies but by his international record: he had caused the United States to be the first country to use the International Court and submitted to its arbitration the long-standing dispute with Mexico; he had himself intervened as arbitrator in the Russo-Japanese war; and he was at that time the only American to have received a Nobel peace prize.

Addressing a convention of National Peace Societies in Boston in 1904, Jane Addams based her plea for internationalism largely on her own experiences of the problems and opportunities of an inter-racial community. Two years later, she was giving a course of lectures on 'Newer Ideals of Peace' at a Wisconsin summer school. The book of the lectures, published in 1907, was widely acclaimed and was twice reprinted in the next seven years. Although her recommendations were never seriously tested, neither were they seriously criticized by any leading thinker. She was heartened to receive the assent of William James to the rightness of her conclusions: Jane Addams, he said, 'inhabited reality'. Such was the optimistic climate of American progressive thought in the years immediately preceding the outbreak of the Great War; years that, for Jane Addams, were filled with honours and distinction.

If her reputation had declined in Chicago during the second decade at Hull House, this was not due to her public connection with the peace movement but to her association with progressive social forces. Nationally, she reached her zenith following the publication of *Twenty Years at Hull House* in 1910. In June that year she was the first woman to receive an honorary degree of Yale university; in October, Smith College granted her the LL.D. The Illinois Equal Suffrage Association urged her appointment to the US Senate; two years later, Boston suffragettes went one better and recommended her as Presidential candidate. Perhaps it was the continual precariousness of her health—at the end of 1909 she had a second serious operation, for appendicitis—that made Jane wary of the smiling face of fortune. As she observed to Florence Kelley shortly afterwards: 'Woe unto you when all men speak well of you'. The prophecy was not to remain long unfulfilled.

NOTES

1 *Twenty Years at Hull House*, p. 29.
2 *Newer Ideals of Peace*, p. 61.
3 'The Subjective Necessity for Social Settlements', *Philanthropy and Social Progress* (New York, Crowell, 1893), p. 18.
4 *Canon Barnett: his Life, Work and Friends*, by his Wife. (London, Murray, 1921). Vol. II, p. 30.
5 See Tolstoy's essay 'Industry and Idleness' *Essays and Letters*, by Leo Tolstoy (The World's Classics: London, Grant Richards, 1903).
6 *Unity* (Chicago), 15th July, 1935.
7 In March, 1901, Tolstoy wrote to Aylmer Maude that he had no advice as to what 'good cause' the balance of the *Resurrection* fund should be allocated: 'so deal with the money as God may put in your heart'.
8 *Twenty Years at Hull House*, p. 420.
9 *Newer Ideals of Peace*, p. 238.
10 *Ibid.*, p. 60.
11 *Ibid.*, p. 35.
12 *Twenty Years at Hull House*, p. 444.

Chapter 7

THE PRICE OF PEACE

In August 1914 a German liner was sighted in Frenchman's Bay off the coast of Maine, close to Mary Smith's cottage at Bar Harbor where Jane Addams spent some part of each summer. The *Kronprinzessin Cecilie* had put into American waters to avoid capture by the Allies of her cargo of bullion. The war was two days old, and this 'huge boat in her incongruous setting', as Jane Addams described it, brought home to the American people the 'incredible news' that France and England were at war with Germany. Perhaps Hull House, with its own bush telegraph to Europe at both grass-roots and diplomatic level, was more awake to the catastrophe than some other sections of United States opinion, still largely isolationist. Jane Addams, at least, was well prepared both in her own personal attitude and in the policies she wished her country to adopt. She was already unreservedly committed to the peace movement; and was to remain committed, in war as in peace, to the end of her life.

Indeed, the impetus to peace that had been rising steadily in the movement through national congresses at Boston and Chicago in 1907 and 1908, continued to gather force inter-nationally right up to 1913, when the Peace Palace was opened at The Hague as a 'tangible pledge' of the substitution of arbitration for war. That same year, Jane Addams addressed a huge audience at the Carnegie Hall in New York—where, two years later, she was to meet with a very different reception —on the 'new internationalism' of the common people. In the summer of 1913, she travelled to Budapest with the American delegation to the International Suffrage Alliance: an experience that was to have repercussions far beyond the limited objective of votes for women. And shortly after the outbreak of the European war, a conference of social workers met in New

York and formed the Union Against Militarism, with Lilian D. Wald of the Henry Street Settlement as chairman. Their protest was directed less against the cruelty and barbarism of war than against its social consequences: the reversal of normal human relationships and the abandonment of the struggle against injustice.

The following January a huge convention of three thousand women assembled in Washington and organized the Women's Peace Party; the conveners were Jane Addams and the suffragist leader Mrs Carrie Chapman Catt, and Jane Addams was elected Chairman. Credit for the organization was actually due, however, to two non-Americans—themselves representing 'enemy' powers and sometimes speaking from the same platform —who the previous winter had appealed to American women to press for peace negotiations: Mrs (later Lady Emmeline) Pethick-Lawrence of England had brought proposals for 'peace aims' from the recently-formed Union of Democratic Control in London, while Mme Rosika Schwimmer of Hungary was campaigning for an immediate conference of neutrals. Mme Schwimmer, then Press Secretary for the International Suffrage Alliance, had already had interviews with Lloyd George and President Wilson, to whom with Mrs Catt she presented an international petition calling for such a conference.

This plan for a Neutral Conference for Continuous Mediation was elaborated in detail by Miss Julia Wales, a Canadian at the University of Wisconsin, and presented to the state legislature; her proposals were approved by both Houses and recommended for adoption to the United States Congress. The Women's Peace Party adopted the plan as the first aim of its eleven-point programme, and issued a call to all international organizations in the United States to support it; as a result, a National Peace Federation was formed following an emergency conference in Chicago in March, 1915, with Jane Addams as President.

Meanwhile, other moves were on foot amongst European women. A group of British, German, Belgian and Dutch members of the International Suffrage Alliance had met at Amsterdam in February 1915, following the abandonment of the Alliance's own conference because of the war, and decided to call an international congress of women to meet at The Hague that April. Its objects would be: that international disputes should be settled by peaceful means; and that the parliamentary franchise should be granted to women. The Dutch Committee, under the presidency of Dr Aletta Jacobs, were given the task of organizing the congress and issuing invitations to all parts of the world. From America, forty-seven women accepted the invitation: amongst them was Jane Addams, who was asked to preside at the Congress and agreed to do so. Many of the European women were already known to her from the earlier Budapest conference of the Alliance, and she had formed the highest opinion of their ability and integrity.

When finally forty-two American delegates set sail in mid-April, 1915, on the Dutch ship *Noordam*—ballasted, significantly enough, by a cargo of wheat—public opinion towards the Women's Peace Party was already veering from approbation to derision. As they approached the English Channel opposition sharpened, and the ship was stopped off Dover while top-level cables were exchanged between London and Washington. Finally, the *Noordam* was allowed to continue to Rotterdam, where the delegates disembarked just two hours before the Congress was due to open. They were more fortunate than their British colleagues, who remained waiting on the quayside at Tilbury for the duration of the proceedings. Out of one hundred and eighty prospective delegates—amongst them women of the distinction of Margaret Bondfield, Eva Gore Booth, Isabella Ford, Sylvia Pankhurst, Maude Royden, Margaret Sackville, Olive Schreiner, Evelyn Sharp and Helena Swanwick—only twenty-five had been given travel permits by the Home Secretary; and on the day they were due to sail, the North Sea was closed to all shipping until further notice. Britain was, however, represented at the Congress by Chrystal Macmillan and Kathleen Courtney, who were already in Holland; and Emmeline Pethick-Lawrence who travelled with the United States contingent.

The Congress assembled on April 28, 1915, with fifteen hundred delegates and visitors representing twelve countries: Austria, Belgium, Canada, Denmark, Germany, Great Britain, Hungary, Italy, the Netherlands, Norway, Sweden and the United States. The French delegation had been refused travel permits by their government. Ten other countries sent messages of support: the Argentine, British India, Bulgaria, Finland,

France, Portugal, Rumania, Russia, South Africa and Switzerland. In the face of ridicule, hostility and danger—some of the German delegates were jailed on their return—the Congress succeeded beyond all reasonable hopes. A series of Resolutions, twenty in all, dealt comprehensively with conditions for the establishment of peace, under the main sections: Women and War; Action Towards Peace; Principles of a Permanent Peace; International Co-operation; Education of Children; Women and the Peace Settlement Conference; Action to be Taken. For immediate action, the vital resolution was number four:

This International Congress of Women resolves to ask the neutral countries to take immediate steps to create a conference of neutral nations which shall without delay offer continuous mediation. The Conference shall invite suggestions for settlement from each of the belligerent nations and in any case shall submit to all of them simultaneously, reasonable proposals as a basis of peace.

Resolutions nineteen and twenty recommended, respectively, that a second women's Congress should be held at the same time and place as the peace conference of the Powers; and that the resolutions of the Hague Congress should be immediately taken by envoys to the rulers of the neutral and belligerent countries of Europe and to the President of the United States. An International Committee of Women for Permanent Peace was formed to make arrangements for the post-war Congress, with headquarters in Amsterdam; its secretary was Chrystal Macmillan and its chairman Jane Addams. To carry out the mission to statesmen the following envoys were appointed: Jane Addams, Emily Greene Balch, Rosa Genoni, Aletta Jacobs, Chrystal Macmillan, Baroness Ellen Palmstierna, Cor Ramondt-Hirschman, and Rosika Schwimmer.

When Jane Addams agreed to preside at the Congress she knew that she had cast her die irrevocably for peace: there was no going back on this. She was aware, too, of what the choice would cost. Above all else in life, she valued the sense of unity with her fellows: a unity that was never more closely knit than in time of war. The merging of the individual with the national consciousness that commonly took place in wartime—and seldom at any other—she held to be 'a high and precious moment in human experience'. But even for that rare experience, war was too high a price to pay. The cost of pacifism, therefore, was the extinguishing of this fellowship at the very moment when it was most certain of attainment; and which, once surrendered in these conditions, might never be regained. In this sense she regarded the journey of the women to the Congress as little less than heroic; for, as she stated in her presidential address at the close of the Congress: 'Even to appear to differ from those she loves in the hour of their affliction or exaltation has ever been the supreme test of a woman's conscience'.

This supreme test had been taken, and passed, in the very act of calling the Congress. The second test, still to come, lay in implementing the decision to differ by means of independent action. And this, the appointed envoys to statesmen now proceeded to carry out. In May and June, 1915, fourteen countries were visited by the delegates, divided into two groups, and in all cases they obtained interviews with heads of states or high-ranking ministers. Jane Addams herself, who travelled with Dr Jacobs and Signora Genoni, spoke personally with eight Prime Ministers or Presidents and nine Foreign Secretaries; amongst them were the German Foreign Minister and Mr Asquith, whom she had met twenty years previously in a London settlement. Jane Addams and Dr Jacobs also had a private audience with the Pope. An account of their reception has been given in the official report of the American delegates:

> We heard much the same words spoken in Downing Street as those spoken in Wilhelmstrasse, in Vienna as in Petrograd, in Budapest as in The Havre.
> Our visits to the war capitals convinced us that the belligerent governments would not be opposed to a conference of neutral nations; that while the belligerents have rejected offers of mediation by single neutral nations, and while no belligerent could ask for mediation, the creation of a continuous conference of neutral nations might provide the machinery which would lead to peace. [1]

Nowhere were the women brushed aside as busybodies or dismissed as ill-informed cranks; everywhere their proposals were closely studied as a possible basis for policy. The mission across war-torn Europe was an astonishing achievement, perhaps unique in history and certainly never to be repeated. We may even—in our present expectation of fifteen minutes to annihilation—envy them a little the leisureliness of their Great War; envy them, too, their own comparative immunity and freedom of movement which was the real justification for their independent action. Jane Addams, as always, was humble in her approach: was it possible for the whole world's statesmen to be at fault, and these few women to be right? One statesman at least believed that it was.

In her own report of the interviews[2] Jane Addams described her meeting with Prime Minister von Tisza in Budapest: 'a large grizzled, formidable man'. Her self-confidence, always precarious, began to ebb and she said to him: 'This perhaps seems to you very foolish, to have women going about in this way; but, after all, the world itself is so strange in this new war situation that our mission may be no more strange or foolish then the rest'.

Von Tisza crashed down his fist on the table. 'Foolish?' he said. 'These are the first sensible words that have been uttered in this room for ten months'. And he explained why. Every day people came to him and asked for more men, more ammunition, more money, because the war could not go on without them. And then the door opened and two women walked in: 'Mr Minister, they said, why not settle by means of negotiations instead of by fighting? They are the sensible ones.'

But still the war rolled on, with an average loss of three thousand men a day on the Western front alone when no military position was changed. Perhaps the women were naive, Jane Addams considered in retrospect,[3] in supposing that 'if the press could be freed and an adequate offer of negotiations made', the war might be over before another winter. From their observations in Europe they were forced to the conclusion that the main factor in keeping the war going was the rising animosity engendered by 'atrocity' stories on both sides; and whether these stories were true or false, they could only increase in numbers and in horrors with every day that the war continued. Europe was slowly strangling itself in its own vicious noose of violence and lies. Everybody, it seemed, was for mediation; and none would take the lead. Inevitably, the smaller countries looked for salvation to the one great neutral outside the theatre of war—the United States of America.

Amongst the statesmen interviewed by Jane Addams had been

President Woodrow Wilson, whom she saw after her return to the United States in August, 1915. He said that he considered the Hague proposals the best formulation of policy he had heard so far; and this in spite of the opinion of his military adviser, Colonel House, that the European ministers had been 'not quite candid' with Jane Addams. At any rate, he was to include many of the recommendations in his subsequent 'Fourteen Points' for a peace settlement in January, 1918, together with the Union of Democratic Control's 'cardinal points' formulated in 1914—to which document the Hague statement was also indebted as a basis for some of its proposals. (For a comparison of the three statements, see appendices at the end of this chapter). Colonel House himself favoured a plan for 'sole mediation' by the United States, although it was known that this suggestion was quite unacceptable to the Central Powers. It may be that the European Ministers had in fact been rather too candid with Jane Addams; and less than candid with the American government—as was to be made tragically plain to Wilson in the negotiations leading to the Treaty of Versailles. But this is to anticipate history.

Throughout 1915 and 1916 there were still some grounds for the qualified optimism of the responsible peace movement in America that, better late than never, common sense and common humanity would prevail before the war situation got completely out of control. The indomitable Madame Schwimmer continued to explore all possible avenues to a conference of neutrals, and in November 1915 she secured a promise from Henry Ford, with Wilson's approval, that he would finance the project. Against the advice of Jane Addams and the Women's Peace Party, the Ford group set about launching the enterprise with all possible speed and publicity. The launching was literally carried out with the chartering of a Norwegian ship *Oscar II*, as a 'Peace Ship' to convey the American delegates to the *venue* of the proposed conference at Stockholm by the circuitous route of Holland, Denmark and Norway. As the day for sailing drew near, the voyage loomed more and more dangerously as a propaganda 'stunt'. Nailed to the masthead of *Oscar II* was the slogan: 'Get the boys out of the trenches by Christmas'. Jane Addams was alarmed, not only that such propaganda was likely to be regarded as treasonable by Euro-

pean governments but that the Peace Ship would be posi-
tively damaging to the far more important enterprise of a
neutral conference. Nevertheless, so deeply did she feel that the
conference must somehow be summoned, that she agreed—to
the dismay of most of her friends—to sail.

The *Oscar II* embarked on December 4th with maximum
publicity. On board were sixty-four pressmen, but not Jane
Addams. She was in hospital in Chicago following a sudden
haemorrhage and recurrence of her spinal trouble; pleuro-
pneumonia set in and she remained in bed for five weeks,
during the whole period of the voyage and subsequent initiation
of the conference at Stockholm the following January. The coincidence did not go unremarked: to some sceptics her illness appeared as a convenient let-out from an embarrassing
commitment. In fact, when Jane struggled from her sick-bed to
attend a conference of the Women's Peace Party in Washington
she collapsed and was taken to California for recuperation.
She did not return to Chicago until the following April, when
tuberculosis of the kidneys was diagnosed and one kidney was
removed. Ford cabled her to come to Stockholm as a delegate,
on which the doctors commented that if she did she would die;
and Emily Greene Balch was sent in her place. Jane Addams
was to remain a semi-invalid for the next two years, perhaps
the most difficult of her whole life; she was then fifty-five years
old.

Meanwhile, the neutral conference was formally inaugurated
with representatives from Denmark, Holland, Norway, Sweden,
Switzerland and the United States. Appeals for co-operation
were immediately issued to neutral governments, and later to
the belligerents. An International Commission was set up,
with headquarters at The Hague, and during ensuing months a
succession of conferences was held in all the neutral countries,
with wide popular support. In October, 1916, Louis Lochner,
secretary of the American Peace Federation and an enthusiast
of the Ford project, returned to the United States full of optimism. The stage was set for negotiation, the players were
ready in the wings, and only one question remained unanswered:
How soon would Wilson act?

Many more people were asking the same question. Wilson
was at that very moment conducting his presidential re-election

campaign on the slogan: 'He kept us out of war'. To the common man, the claim did not seem unjustified. After the sinking of the *Lusitania* in 1915 by a German U-boat, with a hundred Americans on board, Wilson was still 'too proud to fight'. The following March he was rewarded by a German pledge that submarines would not be used against neutral shipping, and that summer Colonel House was in Europe canvassing the possibilities of a 'peace without victory'. The Democratic Party had endorsed a 'League of Nations' policy. Now, if ever, was the moment for the final push for peace. Jane Addams and the peace societies gave Wilson their support, in spite of misgivings about his discrepancies in word and deed, for American foreign policy since early 1916 had become increasingly aggressive: occupation of Haiti, a naval base in Nicaragua, purchase of the Virgin Islands from Denmark, occupation of San Dominica. All this seemed to add up, not to a conciliatory international policy but to control of the Caribbean Sea for military purposes. 'It seemed to us at moments,' Jane Addams commented, 'as if the President were imprisoned in his own spacious intellectuality, and had forgotten the overwhelming value of the deed.'[4]

In November, Wilson was re-elected and Jane Addams attended a celebration dinner at the White House. A month later he sent identical peace notes to all belligerents, inviting them to state their war aims and offering mediation; Germany agreed to attend a conference on neutral ground, but the Allies refused. The psychological moment was perhaps already past; but in January, 1917, Wilson tried again with his speech to the Senate appealing for a peace without victory and offering United States support in a 'League of Peace'. This time, it was Germany that refused the ball. On January 31st she announced unrestricted submarine warfare against neutral shipping around the British and French coasts. Within four days, three American food relief ships for Belgium had been torpedoed and all diplomatic relations with Germany were severed. At the same time, Henry Ford abruptly withdrew his support of the neutral conference—which he was financing to the tune of 10,000 dollars a month—and all hope of a continuous conference to offer mediation was ended.

On March 2nd Wilson made another speech to Congress, and

it was clear that American policy had changed course: 'The world must be made safe for democracy. Its peace must be planted upon the tested foundations of political liberty. We have no selfish ends to serve. We desire no conquest and no dominion. We seek no indemnities for ourselves, no material compensation for the secrifices we shall make.' A delegation to the President from the five leading peace societies came away in complete dejection, convinced not only that war was imminent but that Wilson had entirely repudiated his former pacifist sympathies. Both convictions were almost immediately confirmed. On April 2nd, 1917, America declared war on Germany: ostensibly, in Wilson's apologia to the pacifists, in order to increase her influence at the peace conference and so mitigate some of the worst consequences of the war. This was undoubtedly Wilson's sincere intention, as has been made clear by Mr Herbert Hoover in his recently-published account of these years; [5] and he makes no less clear how far Wilson was duped by the intrigues of his Allies, who by devious means conjured out of his famous 'fourteen points' for peace the dragon-seed Treaty of Versailles. But Wilson was duped also, as Jane Addams at least was soon to recognize, by his own distorted idealism. He had stated in his declaration of war: 'The present German submarine warfare against commerce is a warfare against mankind'. And so, another campaign was mounted in the 'war to end war'! By 1918 he was speaking of his 'contempt' for pacifists, because 'I, too, want peace, but I know how to get it, and they do not'. [6] Nevertheless, he sat at Versailles amongst the victors, and not as the moral umpire he conceived himself to be; yet still believing that his decisions as an impartial adjudicator would be respected, and his democratic principles implemented. Jane Addams, the rejected pacifist, exposed this fallacy:

It seemed to me quite obvious that the processes of war would destroy more democratic institutions than he could ever rebuild however much he might declare the purpose of war to be the extension of democracy. What was this curious break between speech and deed, how could he expect to know the doctrine if he refused to do the will? [7]

Trapped between two half-worlds of idealism and expediency,

G

Wilson was incapable of paying the full price either for peace or war.

If the price of war was a 'victory' that was almost certain to lose the peace, the price of peace was not 'defeat' so much as renunciation: the renunciation of all temporary advantage, whether personal or national, for the sake of salvaging at least some glimmer of hope for the future. This was how Jane Addams came to interpret her role as a pacifist in wartime. Not only the failure of Wilson's policies, but the inevitable distortion of public opinion by war propaganda, made it imperative to carry forward the search for salvation at the level of personal conscience. More and more, in the next four years, she turned for an answer to the traditional function of women as conservers of the race and the application of this function in the post-war world, publishing her conclusions in 1922 in *Peace and Bread in Time of War*. This book is also, more than any other, a record of her own spiritual growth: a kind of prefiguring in one ultrasensitive consciousness of the next stage of progress for the human kind.

Jane Addams had been forewarned of the power of war hysteria to undermine 'normal' standards of reason and common sense, by the reception accorded to the Women's Congress in belligerent countries. The British press offered a fair sample [8] of this: 'Blundering Englishwomen' (*Daily Graphic*); 'Folly in petticoats' (*Sunday Pictorial*); 'This shipload of hysterical women' (*Globe*); 'Pro-Hun Peacettes' (*Daily Express*); 'Women peace fanatics' (*Evening Standard*). Her own first taste of this kind of treatment resulted from her speech at the Carnegie Hall, New York, in July, 1915, when the American delegates reported on their experiences in Europe. She had referred, almost casually, to the many occasions when young soldiers had described to her how before a bayonet charge it was customary for them to be stimulated with intoxicants: the English were given rum, it was said; the Germans, ether; and the French, absinthe. The reason for this—which seemed clear enough to her as an objective observer—was not so much to reinforce the soldier's courage as to weaken his civilized inhibitions, in order that the work of disembowelling might go forward in good heart. To her astonishment, her words were reported as an allegation that 'no soldier could go into a bayonet charge until he was made half-drunk'; and a storm of abuse broke over her in the national press. Perhaps the real motive for the attack, as she herself suspected, was her more pointed accusation in the same speech that the war was an old men's game inflicted on the young, who themselves had little enthusiasm for fighting as a method of settling disputes; although here too she made it plain that she was only reporting what the soldiers had told her, and could not substantiate the indictment. Her impression was, however, corroborated by the flood of letters, bitterly abusive from armchair strategists and mainly appreciative from servicemen, that deluged her for weeks after the incident.

But the real test of conviction came after April, 1917. There was little that the peace societies could do beyond protesting, unsuccessfully, against the conscription that was imposed six weeks after America entered the war; and pressing, also unsuccessfully, for the right of conscientious objectors to exemption, as was granted by the British tribunals system. The only provision made for American objectors was to offer them non-combatant duties, and this concession was limited to members of the historic peace churches—the Quakers, the Mennonites and the Brethren; all others were summarily court-martialled and imprisoned, and their cases did not begin to be reviewed until 1919. By 1916 the Women's Peace Party had a membership of 40,000 and became the United States Section of the Women's International Committee for Permanent Peace, of which branches were then established in fifteen countries. The Section maintained a national office in Chicago throughout the war, even though the existence of such a centre invited public hostility, continual petty annoyances and even obscenities. Jane Addams also served on the board of the Christian-pacifist Fellowship of Reconciliation and warmly supported the Friends Service Committee in its relief and reconstruction work amongst civilian populations: here at last, she felt, was the discovery in action of that long-desired 'moral equivalent to war'.

If Hull House itself came under suspicion from certain quarters during the war, this was less because of the known pacifism of its founder than because of its reputation for sheltering 'aliens'. Although Jane Addams was aware that her own position as a social worker declined—so that it was difficult sometimes to find a chairman at meetings where she was the advertised speaker—the great majority of the residents did not share her convictions and undertook various kinds of war service. And her personal prestige remained sufficient guarantee, at any rate in official circles, that the legitimate activities of the settlement should not suffer; during the whole wartime and immediate post-war period, not a single arrest of an alien was made at Hull House.

Perhaps even worse for Jane Addams to bear than the isolation and misrepresentation of the pacifist in wartime was her realization that pacifism itself, deprived as it was of an adequate means of expression, must degenerate into mere dogma. The conscientious conviction that a cause or a belief was, in some absolute sense, 'right' had never been for her an end in itself, but only the prelude to its application in action. She found little personal consolation in her conclusion that 'a man's primary allegiance is to his vision of the truth and that he is under obligation to affirm it'. [9] Affirmation without works was an arid creed. And by what right, she asked herself, did the individual stand out against the millions of his fellow-countrymen? His justification, in her view, was that he thereby assisted in the evolutionary process: 'as all other forms of growth begin with a variation from the mass, so the moral changes in human affairs may also begin with a differing group or individual'. [10]

This was clearly true in peacetime, as her own experience had shown, but it was difficult to see any possibility of influencing 'the mass' when every initiative was repudiated and every public utterance misconstrued: when she was warned by friends that to persist in pacifism was to commit 'intellectual suicide', so that her judgment would never be trusted again. Nevertheless, Jane Addams did persist—although it is at least open to doubt whether, with her temperamental need for acceptance, she could have continued to hold out without some partial alleviation of her condition of isolation. This came, providentially, in an invitation from Herbert Hoover to assist him in the Department of Food Administration, of which he had been made Director in May 1917. His task was to ensure that an equitable distribution of supplies was maintained for the relief of starving populations in the allied and neutral countries of Europe. Jane Addams had become acquainted with Mr Hoover during his administration of the Food Relief Commission in Belgium in 1915, and was impressed by his devoted service to a cause that was so close to her own heart. If there was one constructive contribution she felt qualified to make in reducing the chaos of war, it lay in the feeding of the hungry. For the nourishment of her personal philosophy, as a woman no less than as a pacifist, no better sustenance could have been offered.

At this point of ministration to human need, on the basis of need alone, all ways to salvation suddenly converged: the rationalization of commerce by government action; the replacement of exploitation by conservation; the utilization of women's deepest instincts; the basis for a new international order of co-operation for the common interest. By the provision of food for the hungry, Jane Addams believed, a new force would be unleashed in the world: a force that might well become a powerful factor in international affairs. Particularly she appealed to women to become the agents of this force; not by deserting their traditional activities, but by extending them to the whole family of man. The appeal, it must be said, fell largely on deaf ears. At a wartime convention of the General Federation of Woman's Clubs at Hot Springs, Arkansas, she recalled many years later, she hoped to find 'some trace of woman's recognition of her obligation to feed the world and of her discovery that such a duty was incompatible with warfare'.[11] The response was not encouraging; but perhaps she sowed better than she knew, for at that very spot twenty-five years later the Food and Agriculture Organization of the United Nations was born.

'What is the matter with the women?', a young soldier had written from the trenches to the Hague Congress in 1915. 'They would not be called cowards and they need not be afraid. Why are they holding back?'

The Congress itself went some way towards an answer. Jane Addams was to go much further, as her search for peace became more and more a search for the deeper springs of human behaviour; in particular, for the springs that both nourished and were nourished by women.

NOTES

[1] *Women at The Hague*, by Jane Addams, Emily G. Balch and Alice Hamilton (New York, Macmillan, 1915).

[2] Published in *The Survey* (Chicago), 17th July, 1915.

[3] *Peace and Bread* (King's Crown Press, 1945), p. 19.

[4] *Ibid.*, p. 57.

[5] *The Ordeal of Woodrow Wilson*, by Herbert Hoover (London, Museum Press, 1958).

[6] *Peace and Bread*, p. 71.   [7] *Ibid.*, p. 65.

[8] 'The Congress and the Press', by Evelyn Sharp, in *Towards Permanent Peace* (Report of the British Committee of the Women's International Congress, August 1915).

[9] *Peace and Bread*, p. 151.   [10] *Ibid.*, p. 140.

[11] *Second Twenty Years at Hull House*, p. 146.

APPENDIX I

UNION OF DEMOCRATIC CONTROL: CARDINAL POINTS ISSUED BY GENERAL COUNCIL, NOVEMBER 17, 1914.

1. No Province shall be transferred from one Government to another without the consent by plebiscite or otherwise of the population of such Province.
2. No Treaty, Arrangement or Undertaking shall be entered into in the name of Great Britain without the sanction of Parliament. Adequate machinery for ensuring democratic control of foreign policy shall be created.
3. The Foreign Policy of Great Britain shall not be aimed at creating alliances for the purpose of maintaining the 'Balance of Power', but shall be directed to concerted action between the Powers and the setting up of an International Council whose deliberations and decisions shall be public, with such machinery for securing international agreement as shall be the guarantee of an abiding peace.
4. Great Britain shall propose as part of the Peace Settlement a plan for the drastic reduction by consent of the armaments of all the belligerent Powers, and to facilitate that policy shall attempt to secure the general nationalization of the manufacture of armaments and the control of the export of armaments by one country to another.

Additional point added May 2, 1916:

5. The European conflict shall not be continued by economic war after the military operations have ceased. British policy shall be

directed towards promoting free commercial intercourse between all nations and the preservation and extension of the principle of the Open Door.

APPENDIX II

INTERNATIONAL CONGRESS OF WOMEN AT THE HAGUE, APRIL 28 to MAY 1, 1915.
RESOLUTIONS ADOPTED

I. WOMEN AND WAR

1. *Protest*
We women, in International Congress assembled, protest against the madness and horror of war, involving as it does a reckless sacrifice of human life and the destruction of so much that humanity has laboured through centuries to build up.

2. *Women's Sufferings in War*
This International Congress of Women opposes the assumption that women can be protected under the conditions of modern warfare. It protests vehemently against the odious wrongs of which women are the victims in time of war, and especially against the horrible violation of women which attends all war.

II. ACTION TOWARDS PEACE

3. *The Peace Settlement*
This International Congress of Women of different nations, classes, creeds and parties is united in expressing sympathy with the suffering of all, whatever their nationality, who are fighting for their country or labouring under the burden of war.

Since the mass of the people in each of the countries now at war believe themselves to be fighting, not as aggressors but in self-defence and for their national existence, there can be no irreconcilable differences between them, and their common ideals afford a basis upon which a magnanimous and honourable peace might be established. The Congress therefore urges the Governments of the world to put an end to this bloodshed, and to begin peace negotiations. It demands that the peace which follows shall be permanent and therefore based on principles of justice, including those laid down in the resolutions adopted by this Congress,[1] namely:

That no territory shall be transferred without the consent of

[1] Resolutions 5, 6, 7, 8, 9.

the men and women in it, and that the right of conquest should not be recognized.

That autonomy and a democratic parliament should not be refused to any people.

That the Governments of all nations should come to an agreement to refer future international disputes to arbitration or conciliation and to bring social, moral and economic pressure to bear upon any country which resorts to arms.

That foreign policies should be subject to democratic control.

That women should be granted equal political rights with men.

4. *Continuous Mediation*

This International Congress of Women resolves to ask the neutral countries to take immediate steps to create a conference of neutral nations which shall without delay offer continuous mediation. The Conference shall invite suggestions for settlement from each of the belligerent nations and in any case shall submit to all of them simultaneously, reasonable proposals as a basis of peace.

III. PRINCIPLES OF A PERMANENT PEACE

5. *Respect for Nationality*

This International Congress of Women, recognizing the right of the people to self-government, affirms that there should be no transference of territory without the consent of the men and women residing therein, and urges that autonomy and a democratic parliament should not be refused to any people.

6. *Arbitration and Conciliation*

This International Congress of Women, believing that war is the negation of progress and civilization, urges the governments of all nations to come to an agreement to refer future international disputes to arbitration and conciliation.

7. *International Pressure*

This International Congress of Women urges the governments of all nations to come to an agreement to unite in bringing social, moral and economic pressure to bear on any country which resorts to arms instead of referring its case to arbitration or conciliation.

8. *Democratic Control of Foreign Policy*

Since war is commonly brought about not by the mass of the people, who do not desire it, but by groups representing particular interests, this International Congress of Women urges that Foreign Politics shall be subject to Democratic Control; and declares that it can only recognize as democratic a system which includes the equal representation of men and women.

9. *The Enfranchisement of Women*

Since the combined influence of the women of all countries is one of the strongest forces for the prevention of war, and since women can only have full responsibility and effective influence when they have equal political rights with men, this International Congress of Women demands their political enfranchisement.

IV. INTERNATIONAL CO-OPERATION

10. *Third Hague Conference*

This International Congress of Women urges that a third Hague Conference be convened immediately after the war.

11. *International Organization*

This International Congress of Women urges that the organization of the Society of Nations should be further developed on the basis of a constructive peace, and that it should include:

a. As a development of the Hague Court of Arbitration, a permanent International Court of Justice to settle questions or differences of a justiciable character, such as arise on the interpretation of treaty rights or of the law of nations.

b. As a development of the constructive work of the Hague Conference, a permanent International Conference holding regular meetings in which women should take part, to deal not with the rules of warfare but with practical proposals for further international co-operation amongst the States. This Conference should be so constituted that it could formulate and enforce those principles of justice, equality and good-will in accordance with which the struggles of subject communities could be more fully recognized and the interests and rights not only of the great Powers and small Nations but also those of weaker countries and primitive peoples gradually adjusted under an enlightened international public opinion.

This International Conference shall appoint: A permanent Council of Conciliation and Investigation for the settlement of international differences arising from economic competition, expanding commerce, increasing population and changes in social and political standards.

12. *General Disarmament*

The International Congress of Women, advocating universal

disarmament and realizing that it can only be secured by international agreement, urges, as a step to this end, that all countries should, by such an international agreement, take over the manufacture of arms and munitions of war and should control all international traffic in the same. It sees in the private profits accruing from the great armament factories a powerful hindrance to the abolition of war.

13. *Commerce and Investments*
a. The International Congress of Women urges that in all countries there shall be liberty of commerce, that the seas shall be free and the trade routes open on equal terms to the shipping of all nations.
b. Inasmuch as the investment by capitalists of one country in the resources of another and the claims arising therefrom are a fertile source of international complications, this International Congress of Women urges the widest possible acceptance of the principle that such investments shall be made at the risk of the investor, without claim to the official protection of his government.

14. *National Foreign Policy*
a. This International Congress of Women demands that all secret treaties shall be void and that for the ratification of future treaties, the participation of at least the legislature of every government shall be necessary.
b. This International Congress of Women recommends that National Commissions be created, and International Conferences convened for the scientific study and elaboration of the principles and conditions of permanent peace, which might contribute to the development of an International Federation.
   These Commissions and Conferences should be recognized by the Governments and should include women in their deliberations.

15. *Women in National and International Politics*
This International Congress of Women declares it to be essential, both nationally and internationally to put into practice the principle that women should share all civil and political rights and responsibilities on the same terms as men.

V. THE EDUCATION OF CHILDREN

16. This International Congress of Women urges the necessity of so directing the education of children that their thoughts and desires may be directed towards the ideal of constructive peace.

VI. WOMEN AND THE PEACE SETTLEMENT CONFERENCE

17. This International Congress of Women urges, that in the interests of lasting peace and civilization the Conference which shall frame the Peace settlement after the war should pass a resolution affirming the need in all countries of extending the parliamentary franchise to women.

18. This International Congress of Women urges that representatives of the people should take part in the conference that shall frame the peace settlement after the war, and claims that amongst them women should be included.

VII. ACTION TO BE TAKEN

19. *Women's Voice in the Peace Settlement*

This International Congress of Women resolves that an international meeting of women shall be held in the same place and at the same time as the Conference of Powers which shall frame the terms of the peace settlement after the war for the purpose of presenting practical proposals to that Conference.

20. *Envoys to the Governments*

In order to urge the Governments of the world to put an end to this bloodshed and to establish a just and lasting peace, this International Congress of Women delegates envoys to carry the message expressed in the Congress Resolutions to the rulers of the belligerent and neutral nations of Europe and to the President of the United States.

These envoys shall be women of both neutral and belligerent nations, appointed by the International Committee of this Congress. They shall report the result of their missions to the International Women's Committee for Constructive Peace as a basis for further action.

APPENDIX III

PRESIDENT WILSON'S FOURTEEN POINTS DELIVERED
TO A JOINT SESSION OF BOTH HOUSES OF CONGRESS
ON JANUARY 8, 1918.

1. Open covenants openly arrived at, after which there shall be no private international understandings of any kind, but diplomacy shall proceed always frankly and in public view.

2. Absolute freedom of navigation upon the seas outside territorial waters alike in peace and war, except as the seas may be closed in whole or in part by international action for the enforcement of international covenants.

3. The removal as far as possible of all economic barriers and the establishment of an equality of trade conditions among all the nations consenting to the peace and associating themselves for its maintenance.

4. Adequate guarantees given and taken that national armaments will be reduced to the lowest point consistent with domestic safety.

5. A free, open-minded, and absolutely impartial adjustment of all colonial claims based upon a strict observance of the principle that in determining all such questions of sovereignty the interests of the populations concerned must have equal weight with the equitable claims of the government whose title is to be determined.

6. The evacuation of all Russian territory, and such a settlement of all questions affecting Russia as will secure the best and freest co-operation of the other nations of the world in obtaining for her an unhampered and unembarrassed opportunity for the independent determination of her own political development and national policy, and assure her of a sincere welcome into the society of free nations under institutions of her own choosing, and more than a welcome, assistance also of every kind that she may need and may herself desire. The treatment accorded to Russia by her sister nations in the months to come will be the acid test of their good will, of their comprehension of her needs as distinguished from their own interests, and of their intelligent and unselfish sympathy.

7. Belgium, the whole world will agree, must be evacuated and restored without any attempt to limit the sovereignty which she enjoys in common with all other free nations.

8. All French territory should be freed, and the invaded portions restored, and the wrong done to France by Prussia in 1871 in the matter of Alsace-Lorraine, which has unsettled the peace of the world for nearly fifty years, should be righted.

9. A readjustment of the frontiers of Italy should be effected along clearly recognizable lines of nationality.

10. The peoples of Austria-Hungary, whose place among the nations we wish to see safeguarded and assured, should be accorded the freest opportunity of autonomous development.

11. Rumania, Serbia and Montenegro should be evacuated, occupied territories restored, Serbia accorded free and secure access to the sea, and the relations of the several Balkan states to one another determined by friendly counsel along historically established lines of allegiance and nationality.

12. The Turkish portions of the present Ottoman empire should be assured a secure sovereignty, but the other nationalities that are now under Turkish rule should be assured an undoubted security of life and an unmolested opportunity of autonomous development, and the Dardanelles should be permanently opened as a free passage to the ships and commerce of all nations, under international guarantees.

13. An independent Polish state should be erected which should include the territories inhabited by indisputably Polish populations, which should be assured a free and secure access to the sea, and whose political and economic independence should be guaranteed by international covenant.

14. A general association of nations should be formed under specific covenants for the purpose of affording mutual guarantees of political independence and territorial integrity to great and small states alike.

PART III

TOWARDS
A NEW CONSCIOUSNESS

Chapter 8

A WOMAN'S PLACE

I<small>F</small> the war had precipitated into general consciousness—as expressed in the bitter cry of the young soldier—Jane Addams own intuitive conviction of the need to restore women to their proper function in society, it had done nothing to facilitate that process. On the contrary, the mounting war psychosis only served to accelerate the crumbling of belief in creative values that a century of unchecked industrial expansion had already sapped in all but the strongest spirits. The women at The Hague were scarcely less representative of their sex than they were of their countries; had they been more representative, their mission would not have been permitted to fail.

Jane Addams was aware of this lack even in 1915, before the worst effects of the war had begun to be felt in America. In *Women at The Hague* she observed that the belief that woman 'as such' was against war could not be substantiated; but that, nevertheless, she feels a 'peculiar revulsion' at the destruction of life. Six years later she was quoted in London as saying, at a reception at Toynbee Hall, that 'the work of reconciliation between nations now and in the future must be done by women'.[1] This was less a contradiction of her earlier statement than a development of it. As in all her thought, Jane Addams extended her vision of the woman's place from the personal to the universal: the instinctive, perhaps misdirected, 'revulsion' of the ordinary, unthinking woman must be channelled into constructive activity.

The revulsion against war was focussed and made coherent in the small group of socially-conscious women who represented the growing point of their generation. It was in part a revolt of realism against the irrelevance of traditional concepts in the externalized, man-made world. Jane Addams' presidential address to the 1915 Congress referred to 'this totally unnecessary conflict between the great issues of internationalism

H

and patriotism'. It was true that far-sighted men had from time
to time tried to rationalize the conflict, to substitute law for
war—she instanced here Grotius, Kant and Tolstoy. But their
appeals had perhaps been made too exclusively to reason and
the sense of justice; and it was to right this imbalance that
women must come forward and play their part:

Reason is only a part of the human endowment, emotion and deep-
set radical impulses must be utilized as well, those primitive human
urgings to foster life and to protect the helpless of which women
were the earliest custodians, and even the social and gregarious
instincts that we share with the animals themselves. These universal
desires must be given opportunities to expand and the most highly
trained intellects must serve them rather than the technique of war
and diplomacy.

As the war dragged on she became more and more convinced
that it was being perpetuated for no rational purpose whatever,
but merely in the service of an outmoded military myth. Only
the Russian peasants on the Eastern front had challenged this
myth when in March, 1917, they laid down their arms to return
to the fields which they believed they could now claim as free
men. They were applying what she called 'the touchstone of
reality' to the slogans of the war; and in doing so, aroused the
baffled fury of the outside world:

Had this myth of our contemporaries that democracy is to be secured
through war so obsessed the Allies that they were constrained to
insist that the troops fight it out on the eastern front as elsewhere,
in spite of the fact that fraternal intercourse, which the Russians were
employing, is the very matrix of democracy? Had war so militarized
and clericalised the leading nations of the world that it was difficult
for them to believe that the Russian soldiers, having experienced that
purification of the imagination and of the intellect which the Greeks
believed to come through pity and terror, had merely been the first
to challenge the myth, to envisage the situation afresh and reduce
it to its human terms![2]

How, in the more sophisticated West, was the myth to be
counteracted? It was little use appealing to the reason of men,
now hopelessly corrupted by false ideals; or to their primitive
impulses which, divorced from the discipline of agriculture, were

almost entirely aggressive and destructive. How was the primitive woman's function—that of nurture and conservation—to be re-established and re-defined? During the enforced inactivity of the war years, caused partly by ill-health and partly by public disapproval, Jane Addams pondered these questions and brought forth some characteristic conclusions. It was in 1916, during a convalescence at Bar Harbor, that she wrote that strangely mystical book *The Long Road of Woman's Memory*, showing how the 'race memories' were passed down from generation to generation by word of mouth, largely through the myths and fairy tales related by mothers to their children. Through this 'ancient kindliness that sat beside the cradle of the race', the challenge to savagery had first been made, and won. In *Peace and Bread*, she invoked the myths of the 'corn mother'—and in Eastern countries, the 'rice mother'—as evidence that in primitive society women were the first agriculturists, as men were the hunters:

. . . in early picture writing the short hoe became as universally emblematic of woman as the spear of the hunter, or the shield and battle axe of the warrior. In some tribes it became a fixed belief that seeds would not grow if planted by a man, and apparently all primitive peoples were convinced that seeds would grow much better if planted by women. In Central Africa to this day a woman may obtain a divorce from her husband and return to her father's tribe, if the former fails to provide her with a garden and a hoe.

Thus, it was the desire of women to grow food, and their insistence that the tribe should not move on until the harvest had been gathered, that led to the abandonment of nomadism in favour of the fixed abode, out of which grew the whole domestic morality of home and village life. In primitive morality, food was shared by the whole tribe, not hoarded by one member whilst another went hungry. It was only with the growth of commercial values that food production—like pottery, clothing and other manufactures—passed out of the hands of women and became a profit-making concern of men. It was never, therefore, strictly true that a woman's place was in the home. Traditionally, her place was in the fields; and it was only as she was driven from the fields by the encroachment of the hunter —whom she had herself converted into a ploughman—that she retreated into the home.

By the nineteenth century, home was all too often very far from sweet, Under the headings of 'Filial Relations' and 'Household Adjustment' in *Democracy and Social Ethics*, Jane Addams analysed in detail the inevitable rebellion of daughters —and domestic servants—as the old, individualistic values collided with new social forces. It is not easy to imagine, in this post-emancipation era, the opposition, misunderstanding and humiliation to which the 'wayward' daughter of the educated classes was subjected in her efforts to serve a larger social end than the wellbeing of her own immediate circle. Custom had so limited a woman's duties to her own family, that 'the woman who stayed at home and the woman who guarded her virtue became synonymous'. All attempts to break away from this restrictive tradition were construed as 'wilful and self-indulgent'. The only acceptable reason why a girl should leave home was in order to set up another home, and to found another family, in the likeness of her own.

Frequently, the sheer drain of moral energy involved in fighting simultaneously on two fronts—against both the mis-construing of her democratic motive and her own natural instinct to preserve the traditional values—caused the rebel to espouse a social cause at the expense of all family claims what-soever. But to adopt a new standard in violation of the old was never Jane Addams' way. At the point of intersection, a second adjustment must be made in order to discover the proper relation between the two. How was such a synthesis to be brought about? To cast off the old claims merely for the sake of personal 'self-development', like Nora in Ibsen's *Doll's House*, was not enough; such an attitude, she felt, could justly be condemned by society. Nevertheless, sooner or later the supremacy of family sanctity must be surrendered in the interests of the general good; just as national sovereignty must be surrendered in the interest of world peace.

The transition from family to communal interest could only come—without destroying the family institution itself in the process—through the acceptance of its wider social function by the family *as a whole*: both men and women, both the young and the old, must voluntarily acknowledge the just claims of a democratic state. To continue to apply the rigidly-exclusive family code in conditions totally different from those in which the code was instituted, was to invite all those personal tragedies arising out of flouted authority and wounded affection. Here again, Jane Addams invoked the example of Lear and Cordelia as a case of failure on both sides to make the necessary adjustment in their relationship.

Already, in war, the right of the state to claim the husband or son of a family was acknowledged. Why then, argued Jane Addams—whilst not condoning the military purpose of that claim—should not the daughter equally be given up to minister to the no less urgent social needs? Even in peacetime, the right of the son to 'make his way in the world' had long been recognized, whilst the daughter was automatically regarded as a 'family possession'. The granting of college education to girls brought the first toehold in the crack: but when the cage door was open, where was the bird to fly? Formal education did not begin to answer the question; if anything, it tended to intensify the conflict between natural affection and intellectual conviction. Training for a career that did not offer some outlet for the emotions was only an exchange of prisons; whilst training of the mind for no other purpose than the acquisition of knowledge was a condemnation to solitary confinement: Jane's own sentence had lasted seven years. She poignantly describes the position of the half-educated, half-fledged young woman that she had known herself to be:

She looks out into the world, longing that some demand be made upon her powers, for they are too untrained to furnish an initiative. When her health gives way under this strain, as it often does, her physician invariably advises a rest. But to be put to bed and fed on milk is not what she requires. What she needs is simple health-giving activity which, involving the use of all her faculties, shall be a response to all the claims which she so keenly feels [3].

It will be clear by now that Jane Addams was not in any sense a 'scholar': the mere accumulation of facts, devoid of human interest or application, could never hold her allegiance. To some extent, therefore, she was ignorant of the joys or the value of pure research, and perhaps failed to appreciate the satisfaction that such activity could provide for the scholarly woman, to the same degree as for the scholarly man—either of whom represented only a tiny minority of their sex.

It may be, too, that she under-estimated the economic factor. If ideals were the pastime of the rich, as brutality was that of the poor, then the latter caused less disruption to society than the former only because its victims had less chance of escape. They had either to grin and bear it; or just not grin. For the educated girl, there was at least the option of lesser or greater evils. But what of the 'labouring classes'? In domestic life as in other areas of living, the choices open to the under-privileged were much more limited; and drudgery by whatever name smells no more sweet. The family tyranny of the working class exerted its grip from early childhood, and less sex-discrimination existed here than in the higher reaches there was little virute in an equality of degradation. 'If you did not keep control of them from the time they were little, you would never get their wages when they are grown up,' one mother remarked to a kindergarten teacher who was advocating a relationship founded on trust. Another said: 'She can afford to be lax with them, because even if they don't give the money to her, she can get along without it'. [4] For husbands, too, the test of domestic virtue was to bring home the pay-packet intact: 'We have been married twenty years and he never once opened his own envelope'. [5] Thus did poverty reduce the human graces of tolerance, consideration and disinterested affection to an expendable by-product of surplus wealth.

Nor did the grip loosen, at least for the daughter, with the coming to maturity. It was still a choice of drudgeries: domestic service, the factory, or a marriage that repeated all the sins and squalors of the parents. The only hope, for such girls, was to make a 'good' marriage: a slender hope, at best, for association with the 'superior' kind of young man who might be thought to provide it was likely to end in disgrace rather than in matrimony. More than seventy-five per cent of illegitimate births in a London hospital, Jane Addams was informed during one visit, were to domestic servants—although she noted that this high figure might in part be explained by the low intelligence and generally inferior background of this class of girl. The brighter spirits went off into the factories and large stores, where monotony and the temptation of attractive baubles led them frequently into the habit of supplementing their inadequate earnings with part-time work in brothels—with or without the connivance of their parents.

In the factory, however, the girl at least had the company of her own kind and the possibility of combined action to improve her lot. She had also the satisfaction of being in the stream of things and expressing in some degree, according to her own character and abilities, the spirit of the age. Jane Addams never condemned factory work as such, but only the bad conditions and anti-social ends of much of this work; and these, she believed, could be ameliorated by education and enlightened legislation. The factory worker, as much as any member of society, had the prospect of contributing to a better social order. The domestic servant, on the other hand, represented the last bastion of feudalism in the twentieth century. No other worker was expected to surrender her private life to her employer to such an extent. If she must be retained at all, Jane Addams considered, the domestic worker should live out, either in her own home or in a residential club. But she found the idea of 'personal ministrations to a normal, healthy adult, consuming the time and energy of another adult'[6] increasingly difficult to reconcile with the practice of democracy.

No progress can come without some sacrifice. And the nineteenth century egress of women from the shelter of the family home took its toll at all levels. At all levels, too, it was the 'domestic ideal' that suffered loss. For the professional woman, the choice of a career meant the almost certain renunciation of marriage and children; she could not have both for several very good reasons:

Men did not at first want to marry women of the new type, and women could not fulfil the two functions of profession and home-making until modern inventions had made a new type of housekeeping practicable, and perhaps one should add, until public opinion tolerated the double role.[7]

For the factory girl, the necessity to work meant the bending of her energies to 'loveless and mechanical labor': labour that was far less rewarding in human terms than the traditional duties of her peasant mother in feeding, clothing and caring for a family. Whilst for the working mother, the ruthlessness of the industrial struggle for survival frequently spelt the ruin of both her own and her children's health. At one extreme, it seemed, the 'great mother breasts of humanity' were totally dried up; at the other, they ran to waste; as in the office cleaner encountered by Jane Addams:

Her mother's milk mingled with the very water with which she scrubbed the floors until she should return at midnight, heated and exhausted, to feed her screaming child with what remained within her breasts. [8]

And babies needed not only milk but love. Long hours of work also deprived the child of that 'tender care and caressing which may enrich the life of the most piteous baby'. Certainly, in such circumstances, the woman's place was in the home; and Jane Addams was an early advocate of state family allowances on grounds both of humanity and social economy.

'Men must work and women must weep' was perhaps never more than a masculine excuse for callousness. Working women at least had always done their share of both; and though that may have been the lesser evil to a life of wretched idleness, it was none the less heroic for that. As the cases which came to Hull House showed over and over again, ninety times out of a hundred it was the woman of the family who, in adverse conditions, kept the home together. The tragic, bitter-sweet story of these lives was unloosed in a torrent of reminiscence by the extraordinary episode of 'The Devil Baby at Hull House', which Jane Addams described at length in *The Long Road of Woman's Memory* and repeated in essentials in *The Second Twenty Years at Hull House*. There was, of course, no such animal as the 'devil baby': he was a figment of the imagination, a creature of myth and memory—no mere fantasy, but deeply-rooted in human experience; this, no doubt, accounted for his longevity. There had been other devil babies in history; the Hull House infant, sustained by nothing more tangible than the breath of rumour, lived for six weeks.

The whole thing blew up one spring morning in 1913, when three Italian women burst into the House and demanded to be shown the Devil Baby. They could even describe him, with his cloven hoofs, pointed ears and diminutive tail; moreover, he could talk as soon as he was born and was 'most shockingly profane'. No amount of denial could disprove his existence, and as rumour added shape to the illusion the stream of visitors swelled to such a torrent that the normal activities of the settlement were almost swamped. From every part of the city and its suburbs the women poured in, from sick-bed and poor-house, from factory and asylum, from all classes and conditions. The legend acquired as many versions as there were nationalities, and as the demand to be 'shown something' became ever more insistent the patience of the residents wore a little thin. Wearily, answering the doorbell or the telephone for the hundredth time in a day, they repeated the unconvincing truth: 'There is no use getting up an excursion from Milwaukee'; or, 'We can't give reduced rates because we are not exhibiting anything'. Some-times disappointment turned to anger, and Hull House was accused of hiding the baby away, of holding out in order to raise the price of admission, and even of letting people believe something that was not true!

Jane Addams confessed that as the farce wore on she became 'revolted' by so degraded a manifestation of an impulse that she conceded to be something deeper than curiosity. One aspect of the episode interested her greatly, however, as she noticed how the 'very old women' seemed to come into their own, to be all at once aware of the rightful heritage of age. It was as if, she said, their minds were stirred by a 'magic touch', loosening the tongues that were so often inarticulate or unheeded and revealing all the accumulated richness of their inner lives. In these revel-ations, she believed, lay the real significance of the devil baby.

In all the variations on the Devil Baby theme there was one common factor: he was a visitation of the sins of his father. The sin might be that of atheism; of cursing the birth of a girl-baby when a son was wanted; or the common one of ill-treatment of a wife. For once, it seemed to the women, the man responsible for an ill-begotten child had met with his deserts: the Devil Baby embodied all the 'undeserved wrongs' of the mother who was afflicted with a feeble-minded or vicious child. Justifiably or not, Jane Addams believed that the theory might at least serve as a marital restraint, there had been a few men amongst the visitors, enquiring rather sheepishly whether the story that the women told was true; and the sphere of marital conduct, she observed, was only second to primitive religion in affording a fertile field for 'irrational taboos and savage punishments'.

The reminiscences of the old women of Hull House showed how thin was the veneer of civilization in primitive family relations. The tragic tales flowed on in a monotone of horror; and of horror so commonplace as to be scarcely distinguishable from the normal standard of conduct: tales of premature births, 'because he kicked me in the side'; of children maimed because 'I had no-one to leave them with'; or dying because 'there was no money to pay for the medicine'. There was the mother whose son used regularly to beat her up in order to extract the money she had earned by scrubbing floors; she could not blame him for copying the example of his drunken father: 'the ugliness was born in the boy as the marks of the devil was born in the poor child upstairs'. And the mother of the wastrel who remarked, with no sense of irony, that although she never reached home from her work of office-cleaning before midnight, 'Joe would open the door for me just as pleasant as if he hadn't been waked out of a sound sleep'.

Truly, as Jane Addams commented, 'we are loved not according to our deserts but in response to some profounder law'. It was because of her acknowledgment of a more profound law than could be encompassed by the rules of reason or common sense, that she did not regard even the most extreme 'love' as folly, or view the appalling experiences revealed to her by these women merely as an indictment of brutality. She recalled with some relish the ballad of the lover whose mistress demanded the heart of his mother as a test of his devotion: the lover promptly cut out the heart and bore it to his lady on a salver; but, stumbling in his 'gallant haste', the heart rolled to the ground and, 'still beating with tender solicitude, whispered the hope that her child was not hurt'. In the light of the 'devil baby' revelations, the story scarcely seemed an exaggeration; symbolically, it was happening every day.

In withstanding the outrages of a cruel world—outrages that were too often inflicted through the agency of their own husbands and sons—such women had continually done outrage to themselves. But Jane Addams does not seem to have regarded this kind of self-immolation as something against which it was possible, or even desirable, to revolt; nor even to have seen

it as excessively heroic. It was no more than a realistic acknowledgment that this was what life demanded, and therefore
the women could do no other. Personal outrage, she implied,
must sometimes be accepted; although social outrage should be
resisted. For, whereas social outrage could be averted by
legislation, in personal terms the best way to eliminate outrage
was by not committing it; and outrages were less likely to be
committed if faced with the counter-force of indomitable love.
It was in this sense, perhaps, that Jane Addams herself reconciled in actuality her Tolstoyan belief in non-resistance with
her active social conscience. The indestructibility of maternal
solicitude she saw as an instance of the great illusion of tragedy:
'that which has power in its own right to make life palatable
and at rare moments even beautiful'. [9]

Woman's capacity for love, as evidenced at Hull House, was
not however limited to husband and children. It was expressed,
for instance, in the devotion of one elderly spinster who for
fifty years had struggled to support a decrepit mother and an
imbecile sister to spare them from the poorhouse or the asylum;
and in the action of that same woman, at the age of seventy,
in leaving her job rather than 'scab' on her fellow-workers by
testifying against the 'ten-hour law' which she herself had
flouted all her working life: a heroic example of the new 'social
ethic' extending beyond the claims of kin. At the other extreme,
lay the attachment of many a prostitute for her 'protector', who
usually cheated and exploited her with complete ruthlessness.
If the scarred hands and mis-shapen bodies of working women
were one kind of monument to the brutality of men—as
exploiters of labour no less than as tyrannical husbands—an
even uglier one existed in the time-honoured institution of
prostitution. Here again, Jane Addams did not waste her
energies in useless condemnation. She had reviewed the
whole subject, with a rare courage and perception, in *A
New Conscience and An Ancient Evil*, published in 1912; a
book which, though outmoded in its terminology, is still far
ahead of its own social thinking.

Prostitution, like slavery, she saw to have had its origins in
the 'loot' of war; and, as with slavery, the only real solution was
abolition. The 'social evil', as Jane Addams defined it, was the
system of commercialized vice that was, and is, permitted to

exist in every great city, whereby 'the chastity of women is bought and sold'; and also, by implication, the chastity of men, since she did not neglect the client in her considerations. She emphasized that she was concerned only with the commercial aspect of the problem, and not with the separate questions of marriage, divorce and 'illicit affection'. She conceded that there might be an 'irreducible minimum' of prostitution in society, as there seemed to be an irreducible minimum of murders. This was a very different matter from the systematic organization of vice for profit—promoted by politicians and protected by the police—that flourished almost unchecked in Chicago until the passing of the White Slave Traffic Act by Congress in 1910. The presence of thousands of uprooted immigrant girls was, of course, a major factor in this particular city; between 1909 and 1912 no less than a thousand 'white slave traders' were driven out, of whom between thirty and forty were known to be 'importers' of foreign girls. The conditions of industrial life, with low wages and long hours of monotonous work, also assisted in sapping the moral fibre of both men and women; as did the deliberate exploitation of the 'human dynamic' of sex by advertising designed to encourage reckless spending in the interests of increased profits.

Although Jane Addams may have set out in this book to discuss only a question of commercial abuse, she inevitably strayed into the sphere of morals that was her natural habitat. For the prostitute, the 'new conscience' demanded that she should be treated by her fellow-women as an object not of censure but of sympathy, and that every effort should be made to restore her to the possibility of normal human relations. And what of the prostitute's client? A moral approach on this side demanded the same standard of chastity for men as for women. The military camp, where men were denied both the rewards and the restraints of family life, represented the extremity of social breakdown. But in ordinary civilian life, much of the demand for prostitutes was artificially stimulated, not only by commercial interests but by the false standards of 'manliness' that were inculcated from schooldays by ignorance and curiosity, unrelated to any general laws of life. One thing at least was clear: that any hope of reaching a modern equivalent of the Roman 'virtue between equals' required a modification of conduct by both sexes.

The women at The Hague, speaking for their inarticulate sisters, might with some justice have tossed back the ball to the young soldier and rejoined: 'What is the matter with the men?' Had they not, by their conduct towards their women, deserved their miserable fate in the trenches? And was not the violence of the battlefield only an extension of the 'normal' violence of domestic and commercial life? They did not ask these questions; not, at any rate, in the voice of Jane Addams. She was sufficiently aware of the impersonal forces in history to recognize that a certain measure of ruthlessness was unavoidable in the progress of humanity from the darkness of the cave and the swamp. This ruthlessness had expressed itself largely through masculine conquest and inventiveness; and with men in charge of public affairs, the emphasis was always too much towards commercial and industrial development, with a consequent loss in human values. It was no part of women's business to put a spoke in this development; rather to counter-balance it by the corrective influence of their traditional care for the preservation of life.

To restore woman to her proper function in society did not mean, of course, that she should cast aside her books and return to the pestle and the hoe. It did require that she should examine the present in the light of past experience and apply her knowledge to those fundamental problems of life with which she was best fitted to deal: 'To control old impulses so that they may be put to social uses, to serve the present through memories hoarding women's genuine experiences,'[10] might liberate new energies and enrich the whole pattern of human culture. Thus might that 'virtue between equals' be attained which involved the common acceptance not only of virtue but—what was sometimes harder—of equality. The forward-looking women of the late nineteenth-century did not ask for restitution or for pity; they asked, more practically, for the vote.

Jane Addams once stated that her interest in women's suffrage was only the inheritance of her father's conviction in the matter. It was true that she never acquired the status in that movement of a Susan B. Anthony or an Anna Howard Shaw, and it was never her first concern. Nevertheless, she was an active worker in the cause and served for many years as a Vice-President of the National American Suffrage Association which fought a sustained campaign before 1914 for state-by-state suffrage; two out of five states thus challenged in 1910 granted the vote to women. At that period, however, most civic activity was channelled through the National Federation of Woman's Clubs: a social phenomenon unique to the United States. Out of an original impulse towards cultural improvement, club activities spread into the fields of child labour, home economics and public health, housing and social hygiene; and out of this concern for social amelioration grew the demand for political enfranchisement. Educated women needed the vote in order to play their rightful part in law-making and municipal administration; humble women needed it for the sake of their children's welfare.

In 'Why Women Should Vote'[11] Jane Addams stated quite simply her own reasons for supporting the suffrage campaign: briefly, the vote represented an extension of tradition to meet modern conditions. It was no longer possible to isolate the family from the rest of the community, and therefore no longer possible for women to discharge even their traditional duties unless they joined in 'the more general movements looking towards social amelioration through legal enactment'. Her conclusion, that women must vote 'to safeguard the home' was less typical of the cause she was pleading than of her personal philosophy. The movement remained in the hands of a small, intellectual *elite*, and the transition to women's suffrage came generally only with the peace. The Victory Convention of the National American Women's Suffrage Association and the first National Congress of the League of Women Voters were held simultaneously in Chicago in 1920.

Before the war, one of the reasons put forward in opposition to women voters was that they would 'infect politics with pacifism': suffrage and peace, it seemed, were as inseparable as two sides of the same coin. For most of the great pioneers of the International Suffrage Alliance and the International Women's Congress, the accusation, if such it could be called, was correct. In 1917 Jeanette Rankin stood up in the House of Representatives and declared: 'I want to stand by my country—but I cannot vote for war'. Twelve years later, the eight women members of the lower House were reported to be in disagreement on all issues save one: that of 'national defense'—and their solidarity was not on the side of pacifism. In recalling this decline in values Jane Addams quoted with approval a saying of G. K. Chesterton: 'Many people have imagined that feminine politics would be merely pacifist or humanitarian or sentimental. The real danger of feminine politics is too much of a masculine policy'. By joining the masculine establishment, women had surrendered their liberty to take the kind of independent action that was possible in 1915. Frequently, too, out of diffidence or the desire for conformity, they failed to maintain in public their own private standards. But when they did have the courage to 'be themselves', as Jane Addams had discovered in her interviews with the foreign ministers, the effect exceeded all expectations; it was the effect, no less, of a new, liberating principle released upon the world.

The coming of peace, and of the vote, brought unprecedented opportunities to test this principle in practice. As never before, the world cried out for succour; the starving, like those earlier supplicants in East London, stretched out their hands for bread. After four years of devastating war, masculine commercial methods like masculine idealism had broken down and proved inadequate to meet the realities of the existing situation. It was with these thoughts, perhaps, that Jane Addams arrived in Paris at Easter, 1919, on her way to attend the second Women's Congress; to tour the devastated areas of France; to search for the grave of her eldest nephew who had been killed in the Argonne a month before the armistice; and to visit Germany at the invitation of the American Friends Service Committee.

NOTES

[1] *Daily News*, September 15, 1921. [2] *Peace and Bread*, pp. 98-9.
[3] *Democracy and Social Ethics*, p. 87. [4] *Ibid.*, p. 45.
[5] *Second Twenty Years at Hull House*, p. 65.
[6] *Democracy and Social Ethics*, p. 113.
[7] *Second Twenty Years at Hull House*, p. 196.
[8] *Twenty Years at Hull House*, p. 174.
[9] *Second Twenty Years at Hull House*, p. 79.
[10] *The Long Road of Woman's Memory* (New York, Macmillan, 1916), p. 114.
[11] 'Why Women Should Vote' (included in *Woman Suffrage: History, Arguments and Results*, ed. Frances Maule, 1915).

Chapter 9

THE POST-WAR WORLD

THE announcement that the Peace Conference would take place
in Paris caused the hasty abandonment of all the pre-arranged
plans for a second Women's Congress 'at the time and place
of the official peace conference'. It had been assumed, in
America at least, that the conference would take place in a
neutral country, probably at The Hague; and the women were
obliged to meet in a neutral country since otherwise their
representatives from the Central Powers could not attend. The
Congress was therefore called, under great difficulties, to take
place in Zurich on May 12, 1919, and in the event it actually
coincided with the enlargement of the Versailles Conference to
admit delegates from the defeated powers.

Whilst waiting in France with the American delegation, Jane
Addams had personal interviews with members of the Peace
Conference and the Food Administration, and joined in a tour
of the devastated regions arranged by the American Red Cross.
Many of the dead were still unburied and she watched United
States coloured troops digging rows of graves to accommodate
the corpses piled high in trucks. She also discovered, on a farm
in the Argonne, her nephew's grave 'the third in one of three
long rows.' A Presbyterian chaplain, only twelve years her
junior, he had written to her:

I shall probably be killed, but if I am not I shall not come back.
There will be too much to do over here that is worth while, and I
should not like the thought of having come to Europe only for
uselessness. [1]

When Jane Addams travelled to Zurich on May 6th for the
Executive Committee of the Women's International Committee
for Permanent Peace that preceded the Congress, she took with
her a copy of the draft Peace Treaty and Covenant of the League

of Nations. The Congress was actually the first public body
to consider these documents, and to pronounce unfavourably on
both. One hundred and thirty-seven delegates were present
from twenty-one countries, both 'enemy' and neutral, and after
four years of war it was found that a certain 'restraint' was
unavoidable in sitting down together at the same table, but
differences were soon melted in compassion as the tragic toll
of war became evident in the faces of the delegates, particularly
those from the defeated countries. An Austrian who had been
present at The Hague, and who was to die from the effects
of starvation three months after her return to Vienna, was 'so
shrunken and changed', wrote Jane Addams, 'that I had much
difficulty in identifying her with the beautiful woman I had seen
three years before. She was not only emaciated as by a wasting
illness . . . but her face and artist's hands were covered with
rough red blotches due to the long use of soap substitutes, giving
her a cruelly scalded appearance.' [2]

The first resolution passed by the Congress, proposed by
Mrs Pethick-Lawrence of Britain, was an appeal to the assembled governments at Versailles to lift the food blockade and
to continue food rationing in all countries until the starving were
fed. This was immediately telegraphed to President Wilson,
who cabled back: 'Your message appeals both to my heart and
to my head, and I hope most sincerely that ways may be found,
though the present outlook is extremely unpromising, because of
infinite practical difficulties'. The President's sympathies were
unfortunately not able to prevail over the French determination
that the blockade should not yet be lifted at any point.

At the close of the Congress, personal emissaries again took
its recommendations on the Treaty and the Covenant to the
'men of power' in Versailles, calling on the Allied and associated
governments 'to accept such amendments of the Terms, as shall
bring the peace into harmony with those principles first enumer-
ated by President Wilson upon the faithful carrying out of which
the honor of the Allied peoples depends'. Once again, they
were ignored, and for the second time, a chance to rewrite
history was lost. Amongst those interviewed by Jane Addams
and delegates from Britain, France and Italy, were Lord Cecil,
Colonel House, Signor d'Orlando and the French Foreign
Minister.

I

The Congress also drew up a programme of educational work and a Woman's Charter, and agreed to set up permanent headquarters in Geneva, the seat of the new League of Nations, in the name of the Women's International League for Peace and Freedom. It appointed as international secretary at Geneva, Miss Emily Greene Balch, a professor of economics at Wellesley College, and elected Jane Addams as international President. In her closing address to the Congress Jane Addams had said:

We shall have to learn to use moral energy, to put a new sort of force into the world and believe that it is a vital thing—the only thing, in this moment of sorrow and death and destruction, that will heal the world and bring it back into a normal condition . . . Whether we fail or not, we know we have the clue, and the military way will have to come to an end, if only because it has tried to do what could not be done except by spiritual power, and so has ruined itself.

On returning to Paris, Jane Addams and Dr Hamilton accepted an invitation from the American Friends Service Committee to visit Germany with a team of British and American Quakers, escorted by Dr Aletta Jacobs from neutral Holland. They were received in Berlin by the German representative for British Quaker work, Dr Elisabeth Rotten. The sight of starvation was no new experience. In Lille Jane Addams had watched a medical examination of schoolchildren:

The children were stripped to the waist and our first impression was of a line of moving skeletons; their little shoulder blades stuck straight out, the vertebrae were all perfectly distinct as were their ribs, and their bony arms hung limply at their sides. To add to the gruesome effect, not a sound was to be heard, for the French physician had lost his voice as a result of shell shock during the first bombardment of Lille. He therefore whispered his instructions to the children as he applied his stethoscope and the children, thinking it was some sort of game, all whispered back to him. [3]

Similar sights were witnessed in Zurich, with the arrival of six hundred Viennese children as guests of Swiss citizens. And now it was repeated in Berlin, in Frankfurt and in Leipzig, where the party saw the feeding of several hundred children with their main meal of the day: a pint of 'war soup' made from meal (often eked out with sawdust) and hot water. All these pitiful children represented only a handful of the European populations—estimated both by Mr Hoover and Sir George Paish, to be one hundred million—who were facing starvation.

Who could act to save them? Only the League of Nations. Jane Addams had hoped and prayed that the League would be founded 'not upon broken bits of international law, but upon ministrations to primitive human needs'.[4] Had it seized this problem of starvation as its special and urgent task, this might have been 'the quickest way to restore divided European nations to human and kindly relationships'. But the League had been set up by a conference of victors, who were content to leave the milk of human kindness in the keeping of the efficient but limited service of the Society of Friends. So was a third chance cast away to lay a firm foundation of peace.

As Jane Addams observed, nationalism was rife in Europe— and nationalism of a more virulent and dangerous kind than anything she had previously witnessed, in 1885 or even in 1915. What had earlier been a force for unity moving in the direction of European federation, as in Italy, Germany and the Pan-Slav movement, was now changed to a splitting and pulling apart of such federations as were already in being. Nationalism had been hardened by war into a dogmatic authoritarianism:

One received the impression everywhere in that moment when nationalism was so tremendously stressed, that the nation was demanding worship and devotion for its own sake similar to that of the mediaeval church, as if it existed for its own ends of growth and power irrespective of the tests of reality.[5]

Whilst inside Russia, the passive resistance techniques of the peasants had given place to a ruthless policy of remilitarization by the Bolsheviks, involving not only an increase of armed forces, but industrial conscription.

Nor, she was to find, was the virus confined to Europe. Back home in the United States that August, Jane Addams and Dr Hamilton faced a fresh barrage of hostility as they appealed for support for the Friends Service Council's fund in aid of German and Austrian children. Not only Germans, but all foreigners, were suspect. American zenophobia inevitably centred on the strangers in their midst, to such an extent that in the winter of 1919-20 no less than one and a half million immigrants applied for return passports to Europe; and most were refused. Liberalism was everywhere in decline, and a noticeable aftermath of the war was 'the dominance of the mass over the individual'.

In the face of this universal reaction towards barbarism, the one pale hope for peace lay in the infant League of Nations. In an effort to infuse a little vitality into the sickly child, Jane Addams campaigned for the 'League of Nations programme' of the American League to Enforce Peace, although the Women's Peace Party was itself still divided in 1920 on the merits of supporting the League. It was also, she found, still difficult for a pacifist to appear on any public platform without jeopardizing the success of the cause, and she was forced to conclude, as philosophically as she was able, that 'to the very end pacifists will occasionally realize that they have been permanently crippled in their natural and friendly relations with their fellow citizens'. [6] Dr Maude Royden, in her memorial address to Jane Addams at St Martin's in the Fields in June 1935, was to confirm this impression:

In America in 1912 I learned that it was unsafe to mention Jane Addams' name in public speech unless you were prepared for an interruption, because the mere reference to her provoked such a storm of applause . . . How well I remember, when I spoke in America in 1922 and 1923, the silence that greeted the name of Jane Addams! The few faithful who tried to applaud only made the silence more depressing.

Nor was the League of Nations itself a popular cause at that time—not, Jane Addams considered, because it was too radical, but because it was tainted with 'the old, self-convicted diplomacy'. It was too closely linked to political and economic self-interest. The one subject the 'big four' at Versailles had tacitly refused to discuss, she noted, was the feeding of Europe.

If the coal, the iron, the oil and above all the grain had been distributed under international control from the first day of the armistice, Europe might have escaped the starvation from which she suffered for months. [7]

Still ruled by the 'old men' of the pre-war world, the League had fallen back once more upon eighteenth century political concepts, 'frankly borrowed and therefore failing both in fidelity and endurance'. [8] They ignored the 'normal motives' of men that were concerned primarily with the satisfaction of simple needs. Jane Addams contrasted the prevarications and shilly-shallying of the League with the simple, concrete proposals put forward by the British Labour Party at its annual conference in 1919.

1. A complete raising of the blockade everywhere, in practice as well as in name.
2. Granting credits to enemy and to liberated countries alike, to enable them to obtain food and raw materials sufficient to put them in a position where they can begin to help themselves.
3. Measures for the special relief of children everywhere, without regard to the political allegiance of their parents.

The first Assembly of the League at Geneva in November 1920, however, brought some measure of hope in the constructive attitude of the smaller nations and the stature of their representatives such as Branting and Nansen. Before the opening of the second Assembly in September 1921, the International Labour Organization was well established and had just concluded a conference on immigration; a subject of special interest to Jane Addams who served for many years as a Vice-President of the American branch of the International Association for Labor Legislation. It was at this second Assembly that Nansen challenged the conscience of the League in his plea for government loans to finance the relief of twenty-five million starving Russian peasants; the appeal was turned down—although in December the United States Congress made an appropriation of 20 million dollars for aid to Russia. And the peasants went on piously sowing their seed that many of them would not live to eat. Out of the self-denial of such humble toilers, Jane Addams believed, a true 'society of nations' might one day be evolved.

The third women's Congress took place in Vienna in July 1921, with thirty countries represented, in an atmosphere of disillusionment and waning hopes. There had been no progress towards 'a permanent peace' as the first Congress had envisaged; no revision of the Peace Treaty as the second had recommended. But every crusade, Jane Addams noted in her presidential address, 'every beginning of social change, must start from small numbers of people convinced of the right-eousness of their cause'. What then could still be done? More and more, it seemed to Jane Addams and her fellow delegates, reconciliation at a personal level assumed importance, as governments continued to ignore all appeals to act in accordance with human need; in particular, the continuation of the food blockade for eight months after the armistice caused a feeling of outrage even greater than that of the war itself.

The work of the national sections of the Women's Inter-national League was impressive in proportion as it seemed to translate theory into action and create a 'propaganda of the deed'. In Britain, following a letter to the *Manchester Guardian* by H. W. Nevinson in December 1919 appealing for rubber teats for German babies' bottles—for lack of which simple commodity many of them were still dying even when milk was provided—WIL members in a matter of weeks had raised £6000 and despatched one million teats to Germany. From Belgium, Mlle Déjardin described the association she had founded for the feeding of German and Austrian children; its members were Belgians who had been deported to Germany for slave labour during the war, and the association had received more than two thousand children as guests in Belgium homes. (A few years later, a group of German women were to make a symbolic gift of trees for planting in the devastated areas of France; they were accepted by the Mayor of Arras for a children's playground.) The Congress—which had set up its own bakery for the feeding of delegates in order not to over-strain the city's resources—saw something of the relief work organized by the Friends Service Council, under the direction of a British member, Dr Hilda Clark; and still, in spite of all efforts for alleviation from voluntary sources, only twenty-one out of every hundred Viennese children, were regarded as approaching 'normal' standards of health.

A certain *rapprochement* was also achieved within the Con-gress. The German and Polish delegates were brought into agreement on a resolution concerning Upper Silesia, and a group from the German section visited the area after the Congress. The English and Irish came to terms on the Irish question—the British section had already sent a mission to

Ireland in October 1920—and a resolution was passed appealing to 'Dail Eireann and to the Irish people that, when their independence is secured, they incorporate disarmament as part of their national policy'. No decision was reached on the official attitude of the Women's League to the League of Nations. The Dutch Section presented an indictment of the covenant and urged that before this could be supported the Versailles Treaty must be revised.

To this end, Jane Addams returned to Europe the following December to preside at a Conference for a New Peace, called by the Women's International League at The Hague, with representatives from one hundred and eleven national and international organizations, estimated to speak for some twenty million men and women in twenty countries. Resolutions called for a world economic conference; the referral of reparations to an international court; and withdrawal of the armies of occupation still in Germany. Once again, Women's International League delegates decided to take these recommendations personally to governments, the envoys being Jane Addams, Catherine Marshall of Britain, and Jeanne Mélin of France. They visited Holland, Denmark, Norway and Sweden, holding a final public demonstration at the Kingsway Hall, London in January 1923. Again, they were ignored.

These journeys formed only the first part of a world tour by Jane Addams, accompanied by Mary Smith, which lasted nine months and included visits to India, Japan, China, the Philippines, Manchuria and Korea. In Japan, she was obliged to undergo a second kidney operation that kept her in hospital in Tokyo for three weeks. She was faintly astonished at the warmth of her welcome in all these countries—so different from the attitude of Chicago at that time. It seemed, she commented, as if 'an internationally minded person should be defined as a friend of every country except his own'. [9]

She summed up her impressions of the tour in a Christmas message to the national sections and corresponding societies of the Women's International League, then representing thirty-two countries. In Europe, she commented, 'baffled and frightened statesmen stand helpless amid a ruined social fabric and see no way out'. Had they never heard of Christ's words, 'Be just and fear not'? It was no use looking to America, which 'abandons the solemn covenants made in her name, restricts her immigration, increases her tariffs, and refuses to consider her war loans as part of an international responsibility'. Perhaps a new leader would arise in the East. She can only have been thinking of Gandhi, whose *ashram* she had visited near Ahmedabad, when she referred to 'the great teacher who more than any other living man is steadfastly committed to the typical Christian adventure, as yet untried, of non-resistance'.[10]

The next WIL Congress took place at Washington in May, 1924, with eighty-five delegates from nineteen countries. Jane Addams again presided, and found it necessary to apologise to the overseas visitors for the unfriendly reception accorded them by a section of the American press. Internationalism, it seemed, was itself a crime to a certain type of 'patriot', though why this was held to detract from love of one's own country was not clear to Jane Addams: 'rather, as Mazzini pointed out, the duties of family, nation and humanity are but concentric circles of one obligation'.[11] The Congress was followed by a two weeks' summer school in Chicago, to which twenty-five delegates travelled in a 'Pax Special' train, holding meetings in many towns en route; although some of these had to be cancelled owing to misrepresentation and hostile propaganda— at Cincinatti, members of the Ku Klux Klan waited on the platform armed with sticks and the train was diverted to another station. The chief focus of opposition, however, came from military circles which objected to statements made in the Congress on the evils of chemical warfare, into which an intensive programme of research was then being carried out.

But the whole decade 1919 to 1929, Jane Addams considered, was dominated by a post-war psychology that was largely conditioned by panic against the 'bolsheviks'. Social progress was slowed down, since the advocacy of any kind of state service was regarded as dangerously close to socialism, and conditions were not improved by the revival of illicit drink rackets under the Prohibition amendment that was in force until 1933.

In 1920 the Civil Liberties Union was founded, with the object of contesting in the courts any attempt 'to violate the rights of free speech, free press and free assembly'; Jane Addams served on its national committee for the first ten years. Isolationism blocked the entry of the United States both to the League of Nations and to the World Court, thereby considerably reducing the authority and efficacy of all international organizations; and this at a time when military spending was increasing everywhere—between 1913 and 1927, she noted, the army budgets of the allied countries rose by two hundred million dollars. That formidable organization, the Daughters of the American Revolution, which had been proud to make Jane Addams an honorary member in 1900 and quick to disown her during the war, drew up a 'Spiderweb Chart' giving the names of fifty black-listed individuals and the organizations with which they were connected. Both Jane Addams and the Women's International League were duly charted here, the indictment against the League being that it was one of two hundred organizations 'operating a world revolutionary movement', or that its members were dupes of such a movement; that it was a factor in the movement 'to destroy civilization and Christianity'; and that it aimed to destroy the United States government.

Also indicted with Jane Addams were Florence Kelley of the Children's Bureau and the labour leader Rose Schneiderman; all three were ably defended by Mrs Chapman Catt, the former suffrage leader (although not herself a Women's International League member) in an 'Open Letter to the D.A.R. which was published in the *Woman Citizen* in July 1927. Jane Addams was also subjected to a vicious attack by the American Legion in 1926, reviving all the old 'pro-German' charges.

Such is the buoyancy of the American spirit, however, that only one year later fifteen hundred people could sit down to a dinner in her honour, organized by a Chicago citizen's committee which included not only social and academic workers but editors, businessmen and even generals. A congratulatory telegram was received from President Coolidge, and it was on this occasion that Charles E. Merriam, Professor of Politics at Chicago University, paid his much-quoted tribute to Jane Addams:

More than any other woman in America she has caught the brooding spirit of the mother and understood how to appeal to what Lincoln called the better angels of our nature. If you say it is not possible

K

for anyone to be at once a statesman without portfolio, a professor without a chair, and a guiding woman in a man-made world, I answer that it is not possible, but—here she is!

Two years later again, in 1929, the fortieth anniversary of the founding of Hull House was celebrated. Its residents now numbered seventy, of whom fifteen had been in residence for more than twenty years and nine for more than thirty years. Its income had risen to 95,000 dollars a year; although Jane Addams' own annual earnings had dropped to little more than a thousand dollars over the past fifteen years. The following year, her own seventieth birthday was honoured at a luncheon given by Mr and Mrs H. J. Morgenthau to seventy distinguished guests, including Francis Peabody of Harvard, Robert Hutchins of Chicago, the British Foreign Secretary Arthur Henderson, and John D. Rockefeller Jr. It seemed as if the triumphs of 1910 were to be repeated; and this time, to be sustained.

The award in that year of the Greek Medal of Military Merit—ironically enough, for services rendered to the Greek Army by the drilling of boys at Hull House to which she had only reluctantly consented—was followed in 1931 by the more appropriate Nobel Peace Prize which she shared with Dr Nicholas Murray Butler, President of Columbia University: a fellow peace worker, who, it was pointed out in some quarters, had suspended his convictions for the duration of the war. Her 16,000 dollars prize money she gave to the Women's International League for the upkeep of its international office in Geneva.

During this same year she was awarded the M. Carey Thomas prize of Bryn Mawr college and chosen by a popular women's magazine as the greatest living American woman. She addressed a conference in Washington on the causes and cure of war, in the company of two naval chiefs, a general and the Secretary of Commerce. And, never forsaking her old convictions for the sake of the new, she became Chairman of the Illinois Committee for Old Age Security, which advocated a system of old age pensions.

In July 1926 Jane Addams travelled to Dublin for the fifth Women's International League Congress, which was attended by 150 delegates from twenty countries; and for the duration of the Congress it was said, peace came to Ireland. It was at any rate notable that delegates were welcomed at the National University by both Mr Cosgrove, President of the Free State, and Mr de Valera, the Republican leader; and although the two men did not meet face to face, the fact that they remained under the same roof together was regarded as an achievement. The Congress was somewhat marred for her by the onset of symptoms of a fresh disease, angina pectoris.

In her opening address Jane Addams paid tribute to the Irish pacifist Sheehy Skeffington, and said:

The Women's International League believes with Mr Skeffington that people are not obliged to choose between violence and passive acceptance of unjust conditions for themselves or for others, but that moral courage and active goodwill will achieve more than violence. We believe that new methods, free from physical violence, must be worked out for ending struggle.

Three years later Jane Addams attended her last Women's International League Congress, at Prague, when she resigned as International President. She was approaching her seventieth year, in indifferent health, weary and perhaps a little disillusioned with organized internationalism. To take her place three chairmen were elected—Emily Greene Balch of the United States, Clara Ragaz of Switzerland, and Gertrude Baer of Germany—and Jane Addams consented to remain Honorary President for life. She continued to give advice and full moral support to the League, as well as generous financial assistance, until the time of her death.

Nevertheless, it is on record that she had been wondering as early as 1924 whether the Women's International League had not, in fact, fulfilled its original purpose, and expressed the view that since women had gained the vote it did not have the same raison d'etre. The fact was, however, that the League was sustained by the enthusiasm of its members, which showed little abatement up to the time of the second world war. Over two hundred delegates travelled to Prague from twenty-six countries in 1929; their main theme was how to implement the Kellogg-Briand Pact for the renunciation of war.

At Grenoble in 1932 they discussed 'World Disarmament or World Disaster', following the world petition to the Disarmament Conference in Geneva bearing twelve million signatures —of which the Women's International League was estimated to have secured half. Jane Addams herself had been appointed as a United States delegate at Geneva, but ill-health prevented her attendance.

The Zurich Congress in 1934 redrafted the constitution of the League in terms that remained unchanged up to 1959:

The Women's International League for Peace and Freedom aims at bringing together women of different political and philosophical tendencies united in their determination to study, make known and abolish the political, social, economic and psychological causes of war, and to work for a constructive peace.

The primary objects of the Women's International League for Peace and Freedom remain: total and universal disarmament, the abolition of violent means of coercion for the settlement of all conflicts, the substitution in every case of some form of peaceful settlement, and the development of a world organization for the political, social and economic co-operation of peoples.

Conscious that these aims cannot be attained and that a real and lasting peace and true freedom cannot exist under the present system of exploitation, privilege and profit, they consider that their duty is to facilitate and hasten by non-violent methods, the social transformation which would permit the inauguration of a new system under which would be realized social, economic and political equality for all without distinction of sex, race or opinion.

They see as the goal an economic order on a world-wide basis and under world regulation founded on the needs of the community and not on profit.

Had Jane Addams been present in Zurich, it is doubtful if such a far-reaching statement of unrealistic aims would ever have been passed. She might well have recalled some of her own earlier strictures on the relation of the concrete to the abstract and the testing of aspiration by experience.

In her farewell address at Prague, sensing perhaps that it was possible for women, no less than men, to become intoxicated with the power of words for their own sake, divorced from actuality, she returned to the strong, simple appeal of her own deepest and longest-held belief. The year previously she had presided at the Pan-Pacific Women's Conference in Honolulu, on which she commented:

There was about this conference and about the session of our own League held after it, a sense of reality, a consciousness of woman's ancient role of food producing versus the primitive food gathering of men which restored, at least to my mind, a confidence which I had lost during the war, that the work of women is nurture and production and must in the end prevail over the mechanistic tendencies of society which make for destruction.

War would never be overcome by resolutions and manifestos, she gently implied, but only by certain countering processes of life. In Western civilization particularly, these processes had become almost completely overlaid by materialistic and mechanistic values. How would the reverse trend be put in motion, if not by her own organization?

By the 1930s there were, it is true, a great many national and international societies having at least some of the same aims as the WILPF. In Britain, they ranged from the League of Nations Union with its support for a policy of 'collective security' to the Peace Pledge Union based on a personal refusal to co-operate in war. It has been alleged, though never proved, that the peace movement of the 1930s helped to bring about the second world war. Rather, it failed in not being able to offer a constructive alternative to war. But the WILPF was still, perhaps, unique in bringing to every fresh situation a consistent and coherent policy.

Examples of this response to changing circumstance in the framework of a continuing principle are given in the booklet *A Venture in Internationalism*. Summing up the world-wide efforts of the 1930s to avert the coming holocaust, the writer comments: 'This widespread determination to put an end to war is a new thing in history'. As we now know, determination was not enough; it had still to be implemented. Jane Addams had shown the way, and her spirit echoes in the pamphlet's concluding words:

This determination, as we well know, cannot be aroused by a mere choice between expediencies, nor made effective by political machinery alone. It demands active devotion to the vision of a world of peace, justice and friendliness, in which life not death is honoured, humanity not wealth is valued, love not hate prevails.

Had the League, in fact, been content to rest on its constitution, it would scarcely have survived a second war and been in the position today to celebrate the centenary of its founder's birth by opening the Jane Addams House for Refugees at Spittal-Drau in Austria, as the special contribution of the League to World Refugee Year[12].

But this is a digression. It may be that in 1929 Jane Addams had both too little and too much faith in the power of the human spirit to reassert its primacy over the most deadening circumstances. As honours and recognition poured in upon her during those last years of recaptured prestige and increasing physical suffering, she was less able to appreciate the merits of the society that bestowed them. Although her love of, and interest in, youth, never diminished, there is evidence that she was not entirely happy in the direction the post-war generation was taking. It was a difference born not of age—Jane Addams was eternally young in heart—but of values. Comparing this generation with her own youth, she found a disquieting acceptance of conformity, especially in college students; although this phenomenon would partly be explained in Chicago by the high proportion of immigrants' children who were now going to college and anxious to appear more American than the Americans. Their conformity was 'a sort of protective coloring'. Along with timidity in the expression of opinion went a devil-may-care 'courage' in the rejection of inhibition, based on half-baked popular adaptations of Freudian theories of repression. Nobody had been more eager than Jane Addams in the preceding fifty years to substitute for Victorian repressiveness a free expression of the whole personality; but she did not find these new forms of expression greatly to her liking. A denial of the value of self-criticism and self-discipline in the interests of 'self-expression' did not, in fact, bring freedom but only a more insidious kind of slavery: 'The fear of missing some emotional stimulus may well become a tyranny worse than the austere guidance of reason'.[13]

Nevertheless, she sympathized with the reaction of youth away from collective and social progress towards individual liberty, and welcomed the greater freedom between the sexes. She was even prepared to acknowledge that such freedom might be a necessary step in social progress towards a new standard of marriage; that the pendulum of change must swing too far before it could achieve a proper balance; and that relativity of moral values was an inevitable concomitant of the physical theories of relativity which were then beginning to acquire—however illogically—an 'absolute' stamp of truth. She only regretted that the 'freedom' for which her generation had fought should now be equated almost exclusively with freedom to experiment at the level of sensation. Was this the 'emancipation' for which women thirty years earlier had suffered and, in some countries, died? Were these women, 'selected by pioneer qualities of character and sometimes, at least, by the divine urge of intellectual hunger'[14] now to be condemned by their spiritual daughters as deluded cranks?

Emily Greene Balch, at any rate, to whom Jane Addams applied for an opinion, did not think so: the fruits of the pioneers, she held, were no mere psychological compensation, but a genuine enhancement to the quality of life all round. They had enjoyed the excitement of taking risks for an unpopular cause; and the satisfaction of proving that they were not necessarily, by reason of their sex, 'weaker and more cowardly, incapable of disinterested curiosity, unable to meet life on her own merits'. They admitted their serious loss in family life, but recognized the value of their gains to society. Miss Balch concluded:

If the educated unmarried women of the period between the Civil War and the World War represent an unique phase, it is one that has important implications which have not yet been adequately recognized by those who insist upon the imperious claim of sex.[15]

It is unlikely that any women's movement of the future will ever again make a comparable impact to that of the suffragette generation. This is not to be regretted in so far as it is a measure of the absorption into the general consciousness of what was formerly held to be a woman's, or domestic, viewpoint. The specialized agencies of the United Nations for the succour of the 'world family' are a standing monument to the extension of this viewpoint into the affairs of men. When a group of over-eager suffragists wished to nominate Jane Addams as candidate for the United States Presidency in 1912 she only laughed; it was one of those immature proposals which are doomed to failure by their disregard of the realities of the social condition. But to visualize Jane Addams as Director-General of the Food and Agriculture Organization is by no means a fantastic proposition; it is perhaps rather more than fortuitous that the centenary of her birth should coincide with the launching of FAO's five-year campaign to 'free the world from hunger'.

But Jane Addams did not live to see this consummation of her life's work. She was too ill even to travel to Oslo to receive her Nobel prize, and most of December 1931 was spent in hospital following another operation. She went to Florida to recuperate and did not return to Hull House until the following April. Perhaps it was her own dangerous illness that turned her thoughts to immortality, for her last book to be published in her lifetime appeared that year; a collection of memorial addresses under the title *The Excellent Becomes the Permanent*. She could not have known that its message was to be tested so quickly with the death the same year of one of her oldest and closest friends, Julia Lathrop. But she had not done with this world yet. Both the Republican and the Democratic conventions took place in Chicago in 1933, and to both parties impartially Jane Addams presented her proposals for necessary reforms: reduction of tariffs, recognition of the Soviet Union, refusal of governmental protection to commercial investments overseas, adherence to the world court, cancellation of war debts, and government control of munitions manufacture. As Linn succinctly reports, 'she got none of them'; though subsequently Roosevelt did accede on Russia and on a *de facto* cancellation of the debts. In 1933 also, she took an active part in the Chicago 'Century of Progress' Exhibition, for which she was appointed 'Honorary Chairman of Illinois Hostesses'; a position that possibly appealed less to her than the honorary Presidency of the World Fellowship of Faiths, which held a congress concurrently with the Exhibition.

The following winter brought a renewal of serious illness which kept her in bed for four months with bronchitis and heart trouble. Her recovery was not assisted by the heavy blow that came in March 1934 with the sudden death from pneumonia of her best-loved friend Mary Smith; in the same house, but inaccessible to her from her invalid's bed. 'I suppose I could have willed my heart to stop beating,' Jane Addams said later, 'but the thought of what she had been to me for so long kept me from being cowardly'.[16]

Her indomitable spirit rallied again, and after convalescence with Dr Hamilton in Connecticut she resumed much of her regular work at Hull House. Honours grew thicker upon her: degrees from Swarthmore in 1933 and Berkeley in 1935; the American Education award that same year. She continued to work on her biography of Julia Lathrop throughout these months, partly in Chicago and partly in Arizona as guest of Mrs Bowen.

In April 1935 she attended a benefit concert for the Hull House Music School and on May 1st travelled to Washington for the twentieth anniversary dinner of the WILPF. She was unable to attend the reception given by Mrs Roosevelt at the White House, but she spoke at the dinner, together with Mrs Roosevelt herself, Congressman Caroline O'Day, Secretary Ickes, Dr Hamilton, Sidney Hillman, Gerard Swope and Oswald Garrison Villard. The next day she met some of her friends who had attended the first Hague Congress in 1915, and the celebrations culminated in an international radio link-up with London, Paris, Moscow and Tokyo. The voices included those of Lord Robert Cecil and Arthur Henderson; Prince Tokugawa; Paul Boncour; Lenin's widow, Krupskaya; with Norman Davis and Josephine Roche from Washington. In replying, Jane Addams put aside her script and spoke directly out of her own heart to the listening world. It was to be her final message, typically selfless; typically unheeded. In it she said:

Nothing could be worse than the fear that one had given up too soon and had left one effort unexpended which might have saved the world.

It was the voice again of the little girl in Cedarville, bearing the sorrows of humanity and oppressed with the realization that 'the affairs of the world could not be resumed until at least one wheel should be made and something started'.[17] Now the wheel had come full circle; and the work must be left unfinished.

She concluded:

The Women's International League joins a long procession of those who have endeavoured, for hundreds of years, to substitute law for war, political processes for brute force, and we are grateful to our friends from various parts of the world who recognize at least our sincerity in this long effort.

She returned to Chicago and resumed her work, particularly anxious to finish her book on Julia Lathrop. On May 10th she attended a meeting of the Cook County Commissioners to discuss the provision of unemployment relief funds. It was the last public duty she performed.

On May 15th she was stricken with acute abdominal pain, and on the 18th entered hospital for an operation that revealed the existence of longstanding, but unsuspected, cancer. She recovered consciousness and lived on peacefully, unaware of her condition, for another three days. She died on May 21, 1935, at the age of seventy-four, a little after six o'clock in the evening. She was buried three days later, after a national lying-in-state, in the 'Addams Lot' of the old family cemetery at Cedarville, Illinois.

NOTES

1 *Jane Addams*, by J. W. Linn, p. 340.
2 *Peace and Bread*, p. 159.
3 *Ibid.*, p. 169.   4 *Ibid.*, p. 90.
5 *Ibid.*, p. 175.   6 *Ibid.*,p. 197.
7 *Ibid.*, p. 213.   8 *Ibid.*, p. 201.
9 *Jane Addams*, by J. W. Linn, p. 356.
10 *Second Twenty Years at Hull House*, p. 173.
11 *Ibid.*, p. 174.
12 Members of the League's eighteen national sections co-operated to raise 30,000 dollars for this purpose. Jane Addams House, comprising 32 apartments, was completed by the end of 1959 and is now fully occupied. A plaque on one of the outside walls bears the inscription from *Newer Ideals of Peace:* 'Not the heroism connected with warfare and destruction but that which pertains to labor and the nourishing of human life'.
13 *Second Twenty Years at Hull House*, p. 194.
14 *Ibid.*, p. 196.   15 *Ibid.*, p. 198.
16 *Jane Addams*, by J. W. Linn, p. 408.
17 *Twenty Years at Hull House*, p. 5.

Chapter 10

THE CROWN OF LIFE

As Jane Addams lay in state at Hull House from May 22 to 23, 1935, in the Bowen Hall auditorium—that was decorated with frescoes of Lincoln and Tolstoy—an unbroken procession of mourners, sometimes at the rate of fifteen hundred an hour, filed past her coffin in homage: old women, children, government representatives, Greek and Italian workmen—men and women of all kinds and creeds who had some tribute to pay, or some thanks to give, for the life of their great neighbour whose parish was the world. A guard of honour stood by, formed from the Hull House Dramatic Association (its oldest society) and members of the Boys' Club. Messages poured in across the world: from the President, from heads of state in Europe, from women's and social organizations, from church leaders and labour unions; even, and how this would have pleased her, from the King of the Hoboes. The Bishop of Washington invited her interment beside Woodrow Wilson in the National Cathedral, but this honour was regretfully rejected in favour of the family grave.

During the weeks following, in memorial services and in the press, assessments of the life and work of Jane Addams reflected again and again the universality of her stature: the broad sweep of her vision and her care for practical detail; her intellectual power and spiritual humility; her greatness as a pioneer in thought and action, that was all but over-shadowed by her sheer 'goodness' of character; above all, her passion for humanity that was never pursued at the expense of any individual being. At the memorial meeting of the National Conference of Social Work on June 10, 1935, Miss Frances Perkins, us Secretary for Labor, commented: 'She really invented social work and social welfare as a department of life in the United States'. This was a tribute to the practical application of Jane Addams' philosophy. Insofar as she could be defined as a sociologist, the whole world was her case-book; and no single human person was ever merely a 'case'.

Many of the social innovations initiated at Hull House have become the commonplace institutions of any civilized country in the world: schools, parks, libraries, health services, all these are recognized as desirable and necessary objects of social policy, however much the means of attaining them may differ. If the status of the 'social settlement' declined in the years preceding Jane Addams' death, this was largely a measure of the movement's success. As she expressed it in her own tribute to Canon Barnett [1]: 'it is openly suggested that they (settlements) have fulfilled their mission and their best friends agree that they have shown their limitations'. For as long as they continued to be needed, settlements were accepted as part of the established order; and those, like Hull House and Toynbee Hall, that have maintained an unbroken growth, have done so by virtue of their adaptability to changing conditions. What better memorial could there be to Jane Addams' original insight in 1889, than the news that in the very month of her centenary a National Training Centre of the National Federation of Settlements and Neighbourhood Centers has been opened at Hull House, aided by a grant of 75,000 dollars from the Field Foundation?

'Plus ça change, plus c'est la même chose'. Conditions change —and over the last century, have changed more rapidly than ever before in human history—but human nature remains very much the same. Three of the most important developments at Hull House in recent years have been in pioneer work with Chicago's 'hard to reach' youth, in clubs for old people, and in community re-development through housing projects. The basic problems remain unsolved: delinquency, loneliness and racial tensions. Close by Hull House are two new housing estates: the Jane Addams Homes and the Grace Abbott Homes. But the Jane Addams children, predominantly Negro, are afraid to cross over into the Abbott grounds where the Jane Addams 'field house' is situated because of white teen-age gangs; and many adults are reluctant to go out at night due to the hostility of their old-town neighbours.

Although we have on the whole created adequate institutions

for social and international co-operation, we have still not evolved the right human qualities that would enable them to function as they should. This would not have surprised Jane Addams. As William James said: she 'inhabited reality'. She knew that although good intentions were of little use without appropriate channels for their enactment, the finest institutions in the world would crumble to dust without the vitalizing power of human impulses and incentives. The need for institutions has been generally accepted; the need to discover the correct motivation of the institutions has not. It is in this sphere, rather than in the practical measures that are necessarily confined in time and place, that Jane Addams' philosophy is still relevant to our present condition; and now, more than ever, needs to be applied.

Another look at the views of some of her contemporaries may offer pointers to this end. It was Oswald Garrison Villard, writing in *The Nation* after her death, who saw in the face of Jane Addams 'the compelling tragedy of Eleanora Duse's aspect'. And yet, he added, one did not think of Miss Addams as a tragic figure. She was always calm and serene, 'concealing, perhaps, deep fires within, as a doctor wears a mask in the face of suffering and death lest he be emotionally destroyed'. [2]

Emily Greene Balch, who followed Jane Addams as President of the Women's International League for Peace and Freedom, and as Nobel prize winner in 1946, carried this analysis further. Jane Addams was continually exposed to suffering—and continually sensitive to it—and this exposure was inevitably printed on her face: 'But I am sure she was very far from being a sad person. She was full of the love of life—of life as it is, not only as it might be'. This love found its expression not merely in her social work but through art, music, and natural beauty. And although her health was always delicate, 'her nervous endurance was extraordinary and the strongest and youngest flagged before she did'. Her 'greatness', Miss Balch considered, had been veiled by her 'goodness':

Men have a curious tendency to turn those of eminent stature into plaster images. Like her fellow-sufferers in this way, Washington and Lincoln, she was a statesman. She was a constructive organizer and builder with judgment of extraordinary penetration and sureness, an original intellect incapable of being trammelled by any formula. Her every action was intrinsic, original, based on the immediate occasion and never an echo of a previous pronouncement of someone else's or of her own . . . She kept no memoranda of her numberless engagements and dates and never so far as I know missed one or was late to one. She operated with no apparatus, as it were, and combined order with an amazing elasticity.'[3]

The greatness of Jane Addams, as a quality distinct from her goodness, was stressed too by Walter Lippman in the *New York Herald-Tribune*. Acknowledging that 'she made of Hull House a citadel of compassion where the dispossessed and the bewildered, the friendless and the forgotten have gone for refuge and refreshment and revival', he went on:

Yet if that were all her life has meant, Jane Addams would only stand in a large company of men and women who in every land and under all conditions are persistently kind to their fellow beings. It is not all. There is something else, which was visible in the beauty of her countenance, was audible in her unaffected voice, is in the style of her writings, and was the special element in her influence. It was the quality within her which made it possible for her to descend into the pits of squalor and meanness and cruelty and evil, and yet never to lose, in fact always to hold clearly, the distinctions that are precious to a maturely civilized being. She had compassion without condescension. She had pity without retreat into vulgarity. She had infinite sympathy for common things without forgetfulness of those that are uncommon.

That, I think, is why those who have known her say that she was not only good but great.

As an exponent of American democracy he compared her to Lincoln: 'Jane Addams was a witness to the ancient American faith that a democracy can be noble, and that serenity and pity and understanding, not merely force and ambition and wilfulness, can pervade the spirit of a strong and of a proud people'.[4]

As with all such witnesses, there was a danger even in her lifetime that Jane Addams would be relegated to a niche in her own 'cathedral of humanity' rather than remain a living influence on the world at large. This point was well expressed in *The Christian Century* of June 5, 1935:

Much nonsense has been written about Jane Addams as 'the angel of Hull House', and an unfortunate amount of it has been repeated in the days immediately following her death. The mistaken purpose has been to establish a traditional figure of the St Francis sort— the figure of a woman who surrendered comfort, ease, all the amenities of life to lose herself in the poverty of Chicago's needy, and to share her crusts as she passed from tenement door to tenement door. The very idea requires a complete misconception of Miss Addams' outlook on life. She had no interest in descending to the poverty level. Her interest was in lifting the level all about her to new heights. For that reason, Hull House under her hand was always a place in which beauty was served, and the emphasis was on the maximum of enjoyment to be extracted from the widest possible spread of human interests and activities. Her 'theory' of social work, if she had a theory, was always to insist that the fullest possible good be required from the working of existing public and social agencies, to demand new agencies when the old had been proved inadequate, and to deal with people on the level of their highest potentialities.

Suffering . . . love of life . . . joy . . . . beauty . . . democracy in action . . . out of all these elements, as instanced in the impressions of her contemporaries, was the greatness and goodness of Jane Addams compounded. It is perhaps rather astonishing, in retrospect, to consider how all these tributes sprang spontaneously, and immediately, to the lips of her fellow-countrymen and women. It is not the war-time rejection of Jane Addams that surprises us, but the degree of her acceptance within her own community, and in her own age. This prophet was not without honour, it seems, in her own land. This is the more remarkable, to a non-American, insofar as we see in Jane Addams so little of what we have come to regard, perhaps mistakenly, as the 'typical' American. Asking the question, 'On what did Jane Addams' authority rest?' a British fellow-worker in the international movement summed up her impressions:

She is not, like so many popular idols, an epitome of the qualities of her countrywomen. American women tend to be restless: Jane Addams is of an exceptionally calm and equable temperament. They are rather excessively exteriorized; she looks inward. They are various, brilliant, occupied with a multitude of tasks; she is simple,

often apparently commonplace, and untiring in the pursuit of her
purpose. She is thus to all appearances far from being the glorified
type of the American woman. And yet she is American to her finger-
tips, and does interpret the real mind and feelings of millions of her
countrywomen. [5]

That this 'other America' of Jane Addams is still with us cannot
be doubted, and its existence offers perhaps the greatest single
hope of world peace—or, should we not rather say, its co-
existence with that 'other Russia' of Tolstoy and Kropotkin,
of non-resistance and mutual aid, that may yet prove to have
been no less indestructible? At least we can say, those forces
will ultimately triumph that are more nearly in harmony with
man's deepest needs and aspirations. And if the needs have
hitherto been typified by the Soviet Union, and the aspirations
by the United States, we can take comfort from the reflection
that, for the making of a whole man, both needs and aspirations must be fulfilled.

Although, as has been indicated, the basis of Jane Addams'
social philosophy is now generally accepted, even where it has
not always been applied, the basis of her pacifism is still as far
from general acceptance as it was in the days of the early
Christians. We have advanced, it is true, to the point of recognizing the need for a 'world consciousness'; and, so pressing
has the need become, have even gone a little way towards
implementing it in cases where our own 'national interests' are
not directly threatened. The token support—compared with the
spending on military budgets—given by governments to the
United Nations specialized agencies testifies to an acknowledgment that, in a world of plenty, human beings of whatever
race should not die of want. The token condemnation—again,
compared with military offensives—of recent tragic events in
Hungary and Suez, Tibet and South Africa, by world opinion
exclusive of the 'aggressors', testifies to an acknowledgment
that moral force may be more effective than nuclear weapons.
But that the corollary of a world consciousness is, quite
literally, as Jane Addams expressed it thirty years ago, 'the
continuity and interdependence of mankind', has scarcely
entered into our thinking at all.

And how, it may be wondered, can so vast and impersonal a

concept ever be comprehended by the common people through whom it must be made effective if it is to have any lasting reality? Jane Addams, it may be recalled, never stopped short at an abstract concept: she related it to a concrete case. She has suggested the answer herself: the world consciousness must be made effective by incorporating it in 'that small handful of incentives which really motivate human conduct'. In other words, the individual, human impulse must be so related to the forces of world development that the two streams flow out of, and into, each other; until they are so related, the conflict of cross-purposes will keep the world, as Hamlet in his time found it, 'out of joint'.

For Jane Addams, her own faculties, temperament and circumstances sustained her thinking at the 'world' level. For the average human being, however, such a range of vision is neither possible nor necessary. Social systems may come and go, dynasties rise and fall, but the ordinary business of living will always remain the chief preoccupation of the great majority of the world's inhabitants. But even this 'ordinary business' requires some extra-ordinary, or super-natural, justification in order to maintain its validity; and so, for centuries, the symbolism of the 'holy family' has epitomized the synthesis of aspiration and need. It entails no great effort of imagination to superimpose on the old tribal and national gods the symbol of the 'world family' with its common aspirations and needs. Within this boundless family—bounded only by a common end —each separate unit can discover its own function and status, and even the 'devil baby' may find a place. For the new philosophy does not break down when confronted with the 'drunken woman' or the 'idiot boy'.

To make this kind of discovery may be as exciting as any trip to the moon. It calls for an examination not only of the ends and means of social policy, but of our own personal motives and incentives. In Jane Addams' understanding—that understanding on which her chief claim to greatness rests—these motives could be reduced to a 'small handful'; and even this handful she saw to have arisen from the primary instincts, in man of the search for food and a mate, and in woman of the nurture and protection of life. If, after twenty centuries of civilization, this analysis sounds simple to the point of naivety, it may be that

L

our imagination has become so clogged by artificial stimuli
that we cannot recognize reality when we meet it. In any case,
the recognition is not intended to be more than a starting-point;
Jane Addams is appealing to us not to forget our roots. Their
ramifications at least are clear enough: invention, discovery
and aggression on the masculine side, opposed or counterbalanced by feminine conservatism, adaptability and dissi-
mulation. This is not an assessment of respective 'merits'. It is
idle to make moral judgments on what are essentially amoral
forces, which lie at the heart equally of art, beauty and religion
as of violence and destruction.

Jane Addams did seek to demonstrate, however, that the
most potent motive forces are those making for cohesion, that
the elements which draw us together are more intrinsic to
human nature than those that throw us apart; and it is insofar
as we express these forces that we contribute to the true destiny
of man. The traditional forms of this expression, as was briefly
indicated in Chapter five, fall into various categories: family
affection, social security, co-operation in labour and re-
creative leisure. At a first glance, this analysis too may seem so
obvious as scarcely to deserve mention. And yet, on consideration, such a conception of the human condition is little short of
revolutionary. It contains all the seeds of that 'self-governing
democracy', built on concentric circles of mutual interest, that
she believed was the only reasonable alternative to the continuing conflict of capital and labour, the continuing maladjustment of the sexes and the continuing power struggle between
nations.

It is a truism to say that the basis of any society is the family
unit; it is also a fact that no successful alternative has been
devised, as the Bolsheviks quickly discovered. In *Democracy
and Social Ethics* Jane Addams had demonstrated that the
family itself must move forward with the tide of social progress;
and that to make this transition amicably the binding impulse of
the family must be a quality of 'affection' capable of absorbing
all the shocks of change—rather than the not uncommon ties
based on security, prestige or domination. As with the Lear of
domestic tyranny, so with the modern industrial Lears: benevolent or not, the despot must give place to the democrat.
'Social security' is an empty shibboleth unless it has the free

consent, and free participation, of every able citizen: security without freedom is the comfort of the grave; freedom without security, the ethic of the jungle.

Co-operation in labour implies a motive of service rather than gain that has never been freely achieved on a national scale in peace-time. It was for this reason, perhaps, that Jane Addams stressed the importance of 'human labor' as the alternative to war: an alternative not only productively, but for the canalizing of physical energy and ideological attachment. While through recreative leisure, freed from commercial exploitation, the craving for 'order and beauty' that is particularly strong in youth could be expressed, as she envisaged it, in festivals of drama, dance and sport. Thus might the 'ideal' world of the imagination be made real; so that, as the Greeks defined it, 'virtue became a free expression of the inner man'. [6] In this sense, recreation would no longer be the antidote to work; work no longer the drudgery to pay for recreation. Through the integration of heart, hand and brain in the satisfaction alike of the highest aspiration and the humblest need, a truly peaceful and creative society might be evolved.

Or was there still something more to be added? Even such a society, if it were to endure, would require some reassurance of its 'moral worthiness' to survive. It was in search of such reassurance that Jane Addams and her generation were impelled into social settlements; that young men were impelled into the trenches in 1914; and young and old impelled to Aldermaston in 1958. The motive for this action may frequently be no more than the desire to feel oneself 'in the right', and self-justification is not an adequate basis for national policy. Although Jane Addams discovered in the first world war that 'a man's primary allegiance is to his vision of the truth', his vision will be no more that a daydream unless he can relate it to the 'truth' of his community. In wartime, Jane Addams failed to communicate her 'truth', and suffered accordingly. This was not, in her case, because she acted out of self-righteousness—'I am never dead sure that I am right', she observed in her report on the interviews with foreign ministers—but in deference to a greater law than those ruling the claims of self or country. Dr Maude Royden revealed the core of Jane Addams' pacifism in her memorial address at St Martin's-in-the-Fields on June 4, 1935:

Most of us when we believe we are in the right, even if all the world is against us, comfort ourselves with the reflection that we *are* right; that other people are insane or cruel or wicked: or, even if we cannot do that, there comes a time for most of us when we have suffered enough, and even the people we love cannot hurt us very much any more. We put armour on our hearts. And it was characteristic of Jane Addams that she could not put on armour—not even defensive armour. This is the very soul of peacemaking, when a person's very heart is not defended, and in this sense Jane Addams was the most completely defenceless person in the world. .

This was the philosophy of non-resistant love—exemplified for Jane Addams by the early Christians, by Tolstoy and later by Gandhi—that was as incapable of inflicting conscious injury as it was able to withstand the involuntary injuries that so often result from the action of love on the unregenerate ego. So rare is this attitude that, although it would undoubtedly be a more effective basis for national policy than a morality founded on self-righteousness, it is unlikely ever to be adopted; this does not mean that its function, as the leaven in the lump, could not be more widely acknowledged and utilized. A society rooted in love need not—in fact, could not—consist only of 'saints' whose allegiance is not to this world; it demands the active co-operation of the ordinary man and woman. Jane Addams never stumbled on Albert Schweitzer's inspired phrase, 'reverence for life', although she expressed his doctrine with every breath she drew. And 'reverence for life' is beyond the reach of no living human being, who merely by existing pays respect at least to his own life.

As war has become impossible, the need to find a satisfying emotional alternative becomes the more imperative: the 'wave of hate' that engulfed the world in 1914, and still has not receded, can only be countered by a greater wave of love. Under the unifying principle of 'reverence for life', new energies could be released in the exploration of character and environment; of human relations in all their aspects; of our relations with the animal kingdom—or with outer space. In such an exploration, no manifestation of life is expendable, and every contribution is unique. It implies one of those 'transformations of man' that were recently expounded by a modern American sociologist, Professor Lewis Mumford, in his book of that name which offers striking confirmation of the prophetic direction of Jane Addams' thought. The time for such a change, he concludes, is now ripe:

The change to One World man was not possible, certainly, at an earlier stage of human development. When the inner ripening had taken place, as it did more than once under the axial religions, the lack of technical facilities and organs of communication alone was enough to impose a veto on the most generous dreams. Again, when technical facilities had brought about physical intercourse on the widest scale, the lack of adequate moral ideas and social purposes largely emptied this intercourse of ideal content and kept it from contributing to the common development. Today, neither the technical means nor the relevant social pressures are absent: it is rather the inner readiness that is lacking. Our generation needs faith in the processes of life sufficient to bring about a willing surrender to life's new demands. [7]

That final sentence might well have been written by Jane Addams herself: it is not the sentiment that is new, but technical developments that have given the sentiment a new urgency.

In face of these terrifying developments, it may be thought that the sentiment of non-resistant love, of reverence for life, or even of surrender to life's demands, is so hopelessly idealistic as to be utterly impractical. In fact, the reverse may be the case, and it is the distorted 'idealism' reflected in the worship of power that may prove itself impractical—as the 'great deterrent' of the H-bomb has already over-reached its possible usefulness. The danger is not that we may overlook the evil propensities of man—but that we may overlook the good. In her memorial address on Sarah Rozet Smith, mother of Mary Smith, Jane Addams made a significant comment:

To be of value in the delicate process of social adjustment and reconstruction, a man must have a knowledge of life as it is, *of the good as well as the evil.* [8]

The italics are mine, and the phrase needs stressing only because it reverses the usual maxim that a knowledge of life is incomplete unless it recognises the existence of evil. Perhaps we do not always affirm this because it is so obvious Most of our institutions are designed to restrain our anti-social impulses, whereas the expression of the impulses to beauty and order is scarcely catered for at all; they are left to make their own way through the jungle, and rarely succeed in reaching the light of day—let alone the sunshine of social approval.

Nevertheless, it is the life-giving impulses that must ultimately triumph. If Jane Addams' priorities in the satisfaction of basic human needs—in the provision of 'peace and bread'— seem unnecessarily restrictive and backward-looking in our present stage of over-development, the restraint is a voluntary one in the interests of a greater development to come. The return to a simpler and more fundamental concept of humanity is not a regression but a necessary turn of the evolutionary spiral. If we cannot make this turn, then we have come to the end of the spiral—and the end of humanity as we have hitherto known it.

If Jane Addams had done nothing more than remind us of our responsibilities for the future of our race, she would deserve to be remembered. She did, of course, do much more; and the present study, which is deliberately limited to certain aspects of her philosophy that seem particularly relevant for today, is necessarily selective and incomplete. A great deal has had to be omitted of the 'human interest' that enlivens the least significant of her reminiscences. Her books, like her life, were at times over-diffuse and inclined to repetition; though never dull, and always responsive to all levels of experience. Even the partial study of such a life has necessarily raised more questions than can be answered within the limits of time and space available in this book. But if it has succeeded, even by raising them, in bringing before our present consciousness those vital issues to which Jane Addams brought a prophet's insight, it will have served its purpose; and, it is hoped, served the memory of one of that small band of immortals who have revealed to us our true nature and end.

There is no evidence that Jane Addams had any belief in personal immortality in the orthodox Christian sense. She was never, indeed, an 'orthodox' Christian; her religion was compounded as much from Greek, Egyptian and pantheist influences as from the Christian Church. (So perfunctory was her attention to formal religion, in fact, that her name was temporarily re-

moved from the rolls of the Congregational church near Hull
House to which she nominally belonged, by a minister who was
irked by her non-attendance! It was, however, later restored and
she remained a member of this church until her death.) But her
belief in the immortality of the soul was not in doubt, and it
speaks through the pages of *The Excellent Becomes the Permanent* with crystal clarity. For this title she made acknowledgment to Plato, and it expresses quite literally her conviction that
in the 'excellence' of a life lies its assurance of immortality:
in the contemplation of such a life (as that of Alice Kellog
Tyler of whom she was then speaking),

our minds are stretched to the measure of the mind of the philoso-
pher who thinks of eternity not as a duration of time but as a certain
quality of the soul which, once attained, can never cease to exist.

By this criterion of 'quality of soul', Jane Addams herself has
won the crown of immortality; and for as long as the human
race continues, her place in human history is assured.

In *The Long Road of Woman's Memory* she referred to the
power of memory in interpreting and 'appeasing' life for the
individual, through the impersonal perspective of time; and its
social value in selecting and transmitting the essential elements
from the past. By means of this transmission, the 'race consciousness' was handed down from generation to generation;
and the content of that consciousness, we might add, deter-
mines its durability. It behoves us, therefore, to give 'excellence'
its due place in our scale of values if we wish to safeguard the
immortality of our own and future generations. In the long
record of the splendours and miseries of mankind, we may set
our own behaviour in perspective and discern that 'continuity
and interdependence' on which our very existence depends;
and which, once perceived, is less likely to be shattered by the
ephemeral and the second-rate. Within this universal humanism,
Jane Addams can speak for us all:

Certain it is that through these our living brothers, or through the
unexpected reactions of memory to racial records, the individual
detects the growth within of an almost mystical sense of the life

common to all the centuries, and of the unceasing human endeavour to penetrate into the unseen world. These records also afford glimpses into a past so vast that the present generation seems to float upon its surface as thin as a sheet of light which momentarily covers the ocean and moves in response to the black waters beneath it. [9]

Whether the light will continue to shine upon the surface, or be engulfed in the black waters of oblivion, it is for ourselves—not Jane Addams—to decide.

NOTES

[1] *The Excellent Becomes the Permanent*, p. 134.
[2] Quoted in *Unity* magazine (Chicago): Jane Addams memorial number, July 15, 1935, p. 203.
[3] *Ibid.*, p. 200.
[4] *Ibid.*, pp. 203-4.
[5] 'Jane Addams, a great internationalist', by Mary Sheepshanks, *Manchester Guardian*, January 12, 1923.
[6] *Spirit of Youth and the City Streets*, p. 20.
[7] *The Transformations of Man*, by Lewis Mumford (London, Allen & Unwin, 1957), p. 190.
[8] *The Excellent Becomes the Permanent*, p. 40.
[9] *The Long Road of Woman's Memory*, p. 168.

INDEX

GEORGE ALLEN & UNWIN LTD
London: 40 *Museum Street, W.C.*1

Auckland: 24 *Wyndham Street*
Sydney, N.S.W.: Bradbury House, 55 *York Street*
Cape Town: 109 *Long Street*
Bombay: 15 *Graham Road, Ballard Estate, Bombay* 1
Calcutta: 17 *Chittaranjan Avenue, Calcutta* 13
New Delhi: 13-14 *Ajmeri Gate Extension, New Delhi* 1
Karachi: Karachi Chambers, McLeod Road
Mexico: Villalongin 32-10, *Piso, Mexico* 5, *D.F.*
Toronto: 91 *Wellington Street West*
São Paulo: Avenida 9 *de Julho* 1138-*Ap.* 51
Buenos Aires: Escritorio 454-459, *Florida* 165
Singapore: 36c *Princep Street, Singapore* 7
Hong Kong: 1/12 *Mirador Mansions, Kowloon*

AGATHA HARRISON

Irene Harrison

Almost by accident Agatha Harrison moved from her earliest post as a kindergarten teacher to become a most influential worker in the vital cause of Anglo-Indian friendship. After welfare work at an English factory, she joined the staff of the London School of Economics as the only university Welfare Tutor in the country. Her great ability was recognized when the American Y.W.C.A. asked her to make the first industrial survey of China for their campaign to raise the living standards of Chinese women.

From her sister's memoir emerges an attractive and courageous personality. Her high intelligence and deep sincerity caught and held the friendship of all sorts of people. Nehru, Rajendra Prasad, Mrs Sarojini Naidu, the British Governors of the States she visited, the factory owners whom she attacked, Sir Stafford Cripps, Viscount Alexander, Lady Mountbatten, are a few of the diverse people who became her friends. Much of her absorbing story is told through her observant and sensitive letters.

Illus. Demy 8vo. 12s. 6d. net

A QUAKER BUSINESS MAN

THE LIFE OF JOSEPH ROWNTREE 1836-1925

Anne Vernon

This is a success story in more ways than one. From a little factory staffed by twelve men Joseph Rowntree's business expanded, in the space of fifty-five years, into a concern which employed over seven thousand people. But the true nature of his achievement cannot be measured by statistics. He was a pioneer in a world where dark shadows from the Industrial Revolution still lingered, and where an "unbridled scramble for the good things of life" was still the policy of many employers of labour. In the uncompromising atmosphere of a nineteenth-century factory he upheld certain traditions inherited from an older and simpler commercial system, and at the same time he anticipated the needs of the future with startling accuracy.

The story of this imaginative business man is told with a lightness of touch which skilfully portrays a Quaker household of the last century, and brings to life part of that history which is still largely unrecorded— the history of firms and factories and the men and women who work in them.

Illus. Demy 8vo. 21s. net

GEORGE ALLEN & UNWIN LTD